Philosophy and Principles
of Auditing

PHILOSOPHY AND PRINCIPLES OF AUDITING

An Introduction

David Flint
Emeritus Professor of Accountancy,
University of Glasgow

MACMILLAN

First published 1988 by
MACMILLAN EDUCATION LTD
Houndmills, Basingstoke, Hampshire RG21 2XS
and London
Companies and representatives
throughout the world

ISBN 0–333–31115–9 (hardcover)
ISBN 0–333–31116–7 (paperback)

A catalogue record for this book is available
from the British Library

Printed in Hong Kong

Reprinted 1991, 1992

'If you suspect my husbandry or falsehood call me before the exactest auditors and set me on the proof.'—Flavius, Steward to Timon, *Timon of Athens* by William Shakespeare

Contents

Foreword

For years a low-keyed debate has rumbled along in auditing and accounting over what 'ought to be'. Practitioners generally argued that theirs was an applied discipline, and meeting the market test was a sufficient requirement. After all, they competed in a free enterprise society; so long as that society was willing to pay for accounting and auditing services, then those services must be filling a real need in a satisfactory manner.

Theorists, generally academics, argued differently. Basing their arguments on carefully constructed rationales, they reasoned to conclusions that sometimes called for substantially different activities and responsibilities on the part of practising accountants and auditors. Occasionally, these arguments had some influence on practice. More frequently, they did not.

In this work Professor Flint has proposed an innovative addition to previous attempts at determining what auditing should be. Rather than accepting present practice because it appears to meet a present need, or preferring some alternative because it is asserted to offer improved service, he has undertaken an exhaustive analysis of auditing from a quite different perspective. Building on Professor Limperg's stimulating 'Theory of Inspired Confidence' and other efforts to establish a theory foundation for auditing, Professor Flint has examined the audit function from the perspective of society in general.

He first asks: What is the role of auditing in society? What is society's need that auditing can meet? Does society expect too much of auditing? In effect, what are the mutual obligations of auditing and society to one another so that society's needs for this service may be met adequately and indefinitely? In seeking answers to these questions, he looks at auditing from the point of view neither of an auditor nor of an auditee, but from that of one whose concern is for the well-being of society, and of auditing as an element in that society.

Approaching his subject of interest from this view leads Professor Flint to a broad view of the audit function, perhaps the broadest view possible:

The social concept of audit is a special kind of examination by a person other than the parties involved which compares performance with expectation and reports the result; it is part of the public and private control mechanism of monitoring and securing accountability.

Proceeding from this broad concept, Professor Flint examines the theory, authority, process, and standards of audit. He does so systematically and extensively. The result is a remarkable addition to the literature of auditing. Here is a work that anyone with an interest in auditing can read and comprehend. The discussion progresses at a conceptual level. The reader comes to understand why the kind of advanced economic society in which we live needs audits and auditors and what that society expects of them. Balanced with those expectations are an inquiry into the real possibilities of audit, with recognition of the limits of its performance. Professor Flint permits neither society to ask too much nor auditing to give too little.

Professor Flint describes this book 'as an introduction to the subject'. Certainly it can be read and understood by those without extensive audit knowledge or experience. But those who complete that reading will have an understanding of the social philosophy in support of auditing as it is performed today and as it must be performed in the future, an understanding that people with much greater knowledge and experience in auditing may never have – unless they also read this book.

R. K. MAUTZ
Editor, *Accounting Horizons*

Preface

The audit process is a well-established institution of a developed society. It is a process on which the members of society call and rely. But like many other social institutions, the circumstances of its creation and the conditions necessary for its existence and continuing development are little understood. The position simply is that these questions have hardly attracted the attention of scholars, and the underlying concepts of this important social activity have not been identified and explored. A notable exception is the work of R. K. Mautz and Hussein A. Sharaf, published in *The Philosophy of Auditing* by the American Accounting Association in 1961. This was a truly seminal work in this field of study. The authors offered it as a first attempt to develop a theory of auditing, recognised that it was both incomplete and inconclusive, but expressed the hope that it would be a possible pattern for research. In 1973, the American Accounting Association published *A Statement of Basic Auditing Concepts* produced by its Committee on Basic Auditing Concepts following a two-year period of research and deliberation. It is only recently (1985) that Limperg's views on audit theory (written in the 1930s) have been accessible to English readers. His basic philosophy shows an interesting correspondence to that of Mautz (who was writing thirty years later), although Mautz was unaware of Limperg's views when developing his own.

Apart from these there has been little contribution to theory development. Research activity has, however, been growing. There has been a number of regular research seminars, for example at the Universities of Kansas, Illinois and Texas; a

Center for Audit Research has been established at the University of Georgia; published papers on audit research issues are appearing more frequently; and academic interest in the United Kingdom and elsewhere is now growing. The research which has been carried out, however, has been directed more to analysis of or to the rationality or theoretical soundness of audit investigatory practices and to the application of other fields of knowledge to auditing practices rather than to the overall philosophy and theory of audit as a social phenomenon.

Mautz and Sharaf, in their work, were primarily concerned with the audit of business corporations and not with the concept of audit in a wider sense, although it would be wrong to suggest that their conceptual approach was not based on fundamental principles of more general application. They also approached the subject in the context of the American institutional, regulatory and cultural environment. In a subject which has strong ethical or moral connotations this is important. Their work is an important milestone in the progress of audit development, but it is twenty-five years since their monograph was written and there have been great movements in social thinking in the meantime.

This book is written from a background of experience of audit practice and academic teaching and research in the United Kingdom. While this does unavoidably influence both the thinking and the presentation, the intention has been to deal with the subject as far as possible on the basis of principles of general application. The audit of accounting records and accounts, for example of business companies and corporations or of governments and other public bodies, may be the most substantial part of present audit activity, but the book is not specifically devoted to this topic. It is concerned with the subject of auditing as a function in society with a number of different applications. It deals with the matter primarily in relation to the public function of external auditing, although some references to internal auditing are made; also, the principles of external auditing will mostly be found to be generally applicable to internal auditing.

Although the audit of financial accounts has been the major application in the past and is historically the most common interpretation of what auditing is, the audit function is now applied more widely and is increasingly embracing non-financial activities and non-accounting data. Even within the traditional area of acounts there is pressure for change as the adequacy of established objectives is challenged. These developments, therefore, give more urgency to the need for some examination and evaluation of the activity, its assumptions, techniques, practices and procedures, and some study of its theoretical foundations.

The book is not intended to be an exhaustive treatise on audit theory. It has been written as an introduction to the subject, firstly outlining the implicit social philosophy and formulating a number of basic postulates from which the theory may be constructed, and then explaining the principles which provide a basis for practice which are derived from the philosophy and postulates.

As the study and preparation for the book have progressed, it has become increasingly clear that an understanding of audit theory – much more a contribution to that theory – requires a depth of understanding in many other fields of knowledge. The inadequacies of the book which stem from the limitations in the knowledge of its author are recognised, but, at the very least, it may stimulate others to do better.

While this book is intended as the basis of theoretical study by those who will later undertake practical instruction and training in auditing, or are concurrently doing so, in which they will be more concerned with practice and techniques which are designed to serve the objectives of auditing, it is hoped that it may also be read with benefit by those who have a responsibility for, or are in a position to influence audit policy-making and audit practice. It is hoped too that it will be read by others who have managerial or administrative responsibilities with obligations of accountability, who are subject to audit, and who wish to have a better understanding of what auditing is about and how it is carried on.

It should therefore be suitable as a basis of study of the subject in general professional, business and management courses in colleges, polytechnics, universities and business or professional schools.

It should also serve to inform those who have to use and rely on audit reports, to provide a better understanding of what assurance they may derive from an audit – and correct much misunderstanding about what has seemed to some to be a dull, routine, mechanical task of uncertain social value. Finally, it may be of value to some social scientists, since the activity with which it is concerned has an important place in the social framework.

The chapters of the book are grouped in four parts. Part I establishes the foundation for the succeeding parts. The audit concept as a social phenomenon is examined and a set of fundamental propositions defining an audit are developed. These provide the framework for Parts II, III and IV, each of which deals with key areas of audit theory. Part II is concerned with the basis of audit authority and examines in detail the subjects of competence, independence, ethics and supervision. In Part III the principles of the audit process are considered in an examination of the nature of audit evidence (when some attention is also given to materiality and audit risk) and the function of reporting and communicating. Finally, in Part IV the standard of technical performance which may be expected of the auditor is analysed to promote an understanding of the level of reassurance which may be derived from the audit.

This is not a large volume, and its objective is a limited one. It has, nevertheless, been a long time in preparation as a consequence of frequent interruptions unavoidably imposed to give priority of attention to successive academic and professional tasks which have arisen over recent years. This delay, however, has not been all loss, as events have served to reinforce developing views and to emphasise the need to stimulate thinking on a more philosophical and theoretical level. In presenting this contribution to understanding of audit philosophy, theory and principles I acknowledge my debt to professional and academic colleagues and friends who have influenced my views over the last forty years. My principal acknowledgment is to Bob Mautz who, while I was still a practising auditor, first stimulated me to think of auditing in philosophical terms, whose writings have influenced my thinking, and who has been kind enough to contribute a Foreword.

Glasgow, January 1987   DAVID FLINT

Glossary

AAA	American Accounting Association
AICPA	American Institute of Certified Public Accountants
CACA	Chartered Association of Certified Accountants
CICA	Canadian Institute of Chartered Accountants
E and AD	Exchequer and Audit Department
FEE	Fédération des Experts Comptables Européens
IAPC	International Auditing Practices Committee
ICAEW	Institute of Chartered Accountants in England and Wales
ICAI	Institute of Chartered Accountants in Ireland
ICAS	Institute of Chartered Accountants of Scotland
IFAC	International Federation of Accountants
UEC	Union Européenne des Experts Comptables Economiques et Financiers

Theory I

Audit: the Social Concept

1

In spite of the social importance of auditing and the fact that it constitutes a significant part of the work of the accountancy profession throughout the world, there has been little interest in the study of its theory or in the development of research. The accountancy profession has shown little intellectual curiosity about a subject which exercises so much of its time and effort. Curiously, scholars in other relevant fields, for example government, corporate governance, finance, or social institutions, appear to have given little thought to auditing, although it is important as part of the machinery of social control in securing the accountability of individuals and organisations of every size and type throughout society, and in establishing the credibility and reliability of stewardship and other financial information.

There is a substantial literature on auditing practice, with the earliest modern text books appearing towards the end of the nineteenth century, and considerable attention is being given to improving and controlling the quality of practice. There has, however, been little interest in or contribution to the development of audit theory. The underlying philosophy is largely taken for granted or ignored. It may, of course, be argued that there is no theory to develop.

A good starting point, therefore, for a book on the philosophy, theory and principles of audit is to consider why it should be thought that there is a philosophy or theory, and what benefit may be expected from developing and studying it.

The practice of auditing has certainly developed without the prior formulation of any theory; and the public conception of the audit phenomenon has evolved without the assistance of a theory. There is, however, no general understanding of what the public conception is or what combination of social relationships gives rise to the situation in which an audit is perceived to be necessary. There is no general answer to the question of what is the purpose of an audit or why the procedures and practices that are adopted are seen to be adequate and appropriate in relation to the perceived objective.

It is frequently represented that auditing is a 'practical' subject, with the inference that auditing is what auditors do, and that it does not have any theoretical content. This view does not stand up to critical examination. There has to be some explanation for society's acceptance of the worth of what auditors do, and of what the audit contributes to the community wealth or welfare. There has to be an explanation of how auditors identify the requirements and expectations of the relevant members of society and how these are interpreted in operational terms, i.e. an explanation of why auditors do what they do, what they believe they achieve, and what the public believes they achieve. There has to be an explanation of the nature, purpose, possibilities and limitations of auditing so that members of society who seek to draw benefit from the function can understand what they can expect to obtain. There have to be some definitional characteristics which differentiate audit from other investigatory, monitoring, reporting functions. There have to be some criteria by which audit performance can be judged and some criteria by reference to which audit practices are adopted. There needs to be some understanding of the nature of the knowledge and the skills that are necessary to practise auditing.

1.1 The Audit Function

An answer can be given to the question of what is the purpose of the audit of, for example, a company or business corporation (although it is by no means clear that the intention of the relevant law is unambiguous, or that it now reflects public expectations), a private firm, a building society, a bank, a state, provincial or local government, a central government department, a private club, and so on. However, that does not tell us what circumstances give rise to these different needs and expectations. Without an understanding of the social expectation it is not possible to know whether the defined purpose or objective in each particular case has been correctly interpreted. Looking at more recent developments, it is by no means clear that there is a common understanding of what is being sought in a 'social audit' or a 'management audit' or an 'operational audit'. Why an 'audit'? What is conjured up by that description of the process which is to be applied, or the function which has to be performed, which would not be conveyed by referring, for example, to an 'examination', an 'inspection', a 'check', or a 'review'?[1]

Most definitions of audit are oriented to a specific situation; they identify the particular objectives and responsibilities of the audit in that situation. One of the more generalised definitions is that of the American Accounting Association (AAA) Committee on Basic Auditing Concepts (1973), that 'auditing is a systematic process of objectively obtaining and evaluating evidence regarding assertions about economic actions and events to ascertain the degree of correspondence between those assertions and established criteria and communicating the results to interested users'. Statements by the professional accountancy bodies are more specific. The first International Auditing Practices Committee of the International Federation of Accountants (IAPC, IFAC) Guideline (1980) states that 'The objective of an audit of financial statements prepared within a framework of recognised accounting policies, is to enable an auditor to express an opinion on such financial statements. The auditor's opinion helps establish the credibility of the financial statements'. The foreword to the Professional Auditing Standards and Guidelines (1980) in the UK states that, 'An audit is the independent examination of, and expression of an opinion on, the financial statements of an enterprise by an appointed auditor in pursuance of that appointment and in compliance with any relevant statutory obligation'. And in the USA the American Institute of Certified Public Accountants (AICPA) *Statement on Auditing Standards* states: 'the objective of the ordinary examination of financial statements by the independent auditor is the expression of an opinion on the fairness with which they present financial position, results of operations, and changes in financial position in conformity with generally accepted accounting principles'. Mautz (1975b) p. 17 suggests that 'the role of auditing in an advanced economic society can be and has been stated in very simple terms – to add credibility to financial statements'.

Describing the auditor's function as expressing an opinion on, or lending credibility to, financial statements or information does not, however, identify the social function or the underlying purpose of an audit. The preoccupation of auditors of business corporations with lending credibility to financial statements and the current emphasis on that function in professional statements is by no means definitive evidence as to the scope of auditing. It is the conceptual quality of the social function which must be understood if the societal expectation is to be interpreted effectively by audit policy-makers and auditors. The general concept of audit and interpretation of its social function do not limit the scope of auditing to accounting data and accountability for financial affairs.

Corporate auditing in its origins was concerned with investigating improper conduct such as error and fraud in accounting. More recent emphasis has been on verifying the information given in the annual accounts. However, current concern with the 'expectation gap' between auditors and users, and public anxiety about the audit of corporate financial management, stimulated, for example, by financial scandals or disasters and revelations of 'questionable' payments, are indicative that the audit function is by no means so narrowly conceived. The development of an operational audit[2] and of a management audit[3] demonstrate clearly the breadth of the field which is comprehended in auditing. In the audit of central government in the UK the statutory basis is over 100 years old and has only recently been modified, but the nature of the process has developed from a simple check of honesty and regularity to a much more sophisticated investigation of economy,[4] efficiency[5] and effectiveness.[6] The theoretical concept of a social audit,[7] however ill-defined the practice may yet be, is perhaps the most striking evidence that 'lending credibility to financial statements' is only one manifestation of the social function of auditing, although, no doubt, a very important one.

It is important that in an endeavour to conceptualise the social function, the objective of lending credibility to financial statements should be seen in perspective. The matter that is under investigation and on which judgement is being exercised and opinion formed in the cases cited is the quality of conduct of individuals and organisations measured against some social norms. Concerned as it is with standards of conduct, the basic issue in auditing is an ethical one.

An ethical base

It is for society to determine what are the norms of conduct in different organisations, and which aspects of accountability have to be subject to the scrutiny of audit. Since ethics in business, administration and public life can be expected to have some relationship with the ethics of members of society in private life, an understanding of this relationship is fundamental to policy-making in auditing.

It is basically the business or public ethic which the audit seeks to monitor. While the concept of audit may remain constant, the operational interpretation of the concept is an evolving one, dependent not only on changing ethical values but also on a societal value judgement as to those issues of accountability to which the audit process should be applied, as the social benefit is perceived to exceed the relative social cost. Changing circumstances, either of ethical standards or of societal needs, determine the evolution of the audit.

There are, however, differing views on the ethics of business and public life. What do the interest groups to whom the auditor reports expect? Questionable practices which stop short of fraud or illegality are difficult to define; and different societies have different criteria. Are the auditors to act as the corporate or public conscience on these matters? Reporting on a Symposium on Ethics in Corporate Financial Reporting, Burton (1972) recounts:

> **There was also considerable discussion related to the distinction between ethical and legal standards for defining good practice in the reporting sphere. Some participants felt that only through the development of legal standards and enforcement through the legal process could sound ethical practice be satisfactorily**

achieved. They pointed out that once ethical standards became norms they would be applied by the courts and would become part of the legal structure of the reporting environment. Recent cases and decisions have supported the view that where professional standards lag behind public expectations, the latter may serve as the basis for determining both legal liability and ethical judgments as to what represents the proper course of action. (Burton, 1972, p. 49)

The relevance of the interaction of ethical standards, relative social benefits and changing importance or nature of environmental circumstances can be discerned in the evolution of audit in both the private and public sectors. An audit of honesty, legality, regularity and accurate (sic) accounting in business on a voluntary basis in the interests of shareholders in the nineteenth century has evolved in response to these social pressures to the current legal one in which the primary emphasis, rightly or wrongly, is claimed to be in endorsing the view given by accounts, in which it is acknowledged a range of users are interested. Development of the concepts of operational audit and management audit are further illustrations of the operation of the interaction of ethical standards, social values and environmental circumstances to develop the audit to monitor conduct and performance as measured against the perceived norms. More significantly, the concept of social audit of business has emerged as an expression of society's concern, and this development is a very clear manifestation of the interaction to which attention is being drawn. There has been evolution in the public sector, too, which is confirmed by the Government Green Paper (1980) which stated explicitly: 'neither the 1866 nor the 1921 E and A D Acts specifically provide for him [the Comptroller and Auditor General] to examine broader questions of efficiency and economy or of effectiveness, but since they do not provide any detailed guidance on the scope of the audit, it has been possible for changes to take place without the need for amending legislation'; and the thrust of the pressure for further development is in the area of the effectiveness audit, 'to assess whether programmes or projects undertaken to meet established policy goals or objectives have met those aims'.

The standards or criteria of accountability which are set by society define the expectation of performance, and the audit undoubtedly fulfils a social function in investigating and reporting on achievement. The really onerous social responsibility of audit, however, derives from the fact that these standards and criteria are to a greater or lesser extent subjective and are continually evolving. The social responsibility of the audit is to interpret dynamically, and not statically and inflexibly, the meaning and thus the expectation of the audit requirement which is imposed by law or by agreement in a particular set of circumstances.

1.2 The Audit Concept

There is, therefore, a place for theory to explain the responsibility of the audit function and the basis of its evolution, and to assist in resolving the unanswered questions which have been posed – not a theory built up on a piecemeal basis from a series of solutions to particular questions, but a set of comprehensive propositions making up an overall theory from which the solutions to all these questions can be derived. As Mautz and Sharaf (1961) suggest, auditing has 'reached a state of maturity at which it will do well to pause for a bit of introspection and to take stock of its presuppositions, aims and methods'. They go on to state: 'No special subject can make real progress until its basic assumptions, their nature, weaknesses, and implications are uncovered and examined.' They also claim: 'As auditing has increased in importance, the work of the auditor has come to touch upon some of the more important aspects of contemporary society . . . Yet its underlying assumptions have not been brought forth for scrutiny and evaluation.'

The purpose of theory in relation to auditing is to provide a coherent set of propositions about the activity which explains its social purpose and objectives, which furnishes a rational foundation and justification for its practices and procedures, relating them to the purposes and objectives, and which explains the place of the activity in the context of the institutions of society and the social, economic and political environment.

Conceptualising about auditing is and has been inhibited by the narrow perception of the scope of auditing by most of those who are knowledgeable about its practice. There is evidence of a widespread difficulty in seeing that the present specific objectives are the current manifestations of a deeper purpose: a preoccupation with accounting number-oriented auditing has obscured a realisation that the social purpose of auditing may be served by the use of other criteria: and a commitment to long-established bases of reviewing the performance of individuals and organisations has caused difficulty in adjusting to changes in social attitudes and expectations. To develop a theory that will stand up to the test of time in evolving society it is necessary to look very much deeper, and to take a more fundamental and radical approach.

A scientific approach to the formulation of *a priori* hypotheses about audit theory requires observation and investigation of the audit process over time. The practice procedures and specific objectives may have changed, but the purpose of the observation and investigation is to find out what there is in the fundamental concept which has remained constant. Whatever the extent of change, there must be some minimum continuing constant element which constitutes what can be identified and described as the 'audit'. A scientific approach requires also investigation of the societal factors, the cultural, legal, social, economic and political influences and constraints, which condition society's perception of the audit purpose and objective.

The need for such investigation is clear from the growing evidence of uncertainty and dissatisfaction about the purpose and objective of current auditing practice. In the United Kingdom, this has found expression in press comment and, more authoritatively, in the reports of the Department of Trade Inspectors about failures of comprehension and unwarranted expectations of the audit process in both the public and private sectors of the economy. In reporting on their investigation into the affairs of Peachey Property Corporation Ltd, the Inspectors (1979) state in relation to the functions of auditors: 'It seems to us that many of the criticisms which we have encountered stem from an imperfect understanding of the functions of auditors both as laid down by statute and as understood by the auditing profession.' In North America, in particular, concern about 'the expectation gap' is well documented by both professional and governmental enquiries; the Cohen Commission (AICPA, 1978), for example, concluded that 'After considerable study of available evidence and its own research . . . such a gap [a gap between the performance of auditors and the expectations of the users of financial statements] does exist'; the Adams Committee (CICA, 1978) found that 'There seems to be a gap between what the public expects and what auditors are doing'; and the Metcalf Committee (1978) asserted that 'The pattern of conduct followed by independent auditors and the scope of services they offer must be reexamined to determine whether they are compatible with public expectations'. Some eight years later the Anderson Committee (AICPA, 1986) reported in a section headed 'Public Expectation Gap' that 'Although significant changes have been made in auditing standards since the issuance of that report [The Cohen Commission] to state the auditor's responsibility in this area more positively, public expectations are not fully satisfied by the level of responsibility assumed', and quoted from an address by the chairman of the Public Oversight Board:

The cause of the crisis is a fact that investors and depositors are losing faith in the ability of the accounting profession to perform the job which has historically been its unique function in our society – assuring the integrity of the financial information upon which our capitalistic society necessarily depends.

There is evidence of public concern about what is being achieved in the audit of accounting and financial statements. The Cohen Commission (AICPA, 1978, p. 57) took the view that: 'In the immediate future, it would be unreasonable to expect the audit function to include information routinely that is largely based on disciplines other than accounting.' There are indications, however, that there are pressures from some quarters for a different kind of audit, for example for an 'operational audit' or a 'management audit' in which the measures of performance involve a number of disciplines for which a variety of experts would be required. In the United Kingdom, particularly in the public sector, there is an increasing interest in the audit of 'value for money', a general descriptive term for audits directed to examining economy, efficiency and effectiveness. There is increasing support also for the claims of those who would demand 'a social audit' to report on the social behaviour and performance of organisations in all their relationships with society, individuals and other organisations.

While this helps in the search for a theoretical starting point, it also poses a problem. By demonstrating a desire to extend the particular process to additional activities, it confirms that there is a publicly held view of the audit concept; but lack of specification and definition makes it impossible at this stage to judge whether the type of investigation and report which users are seeking is one which theoretically conforms to the concept of audit, or which, in terms of practicality, can do so.

Accountability

The audit function and purpose are sometimes explained by saying that an audit is required where there is a duty of accountability between two parties, or between one party and a number of other parties, and that an audit is the means by which accountability is ensured. Audit is a control mechanism to monitor conduct and performance, and to secure or enforce accountability. Gilling (1976, p. 100) develops the argument for this view, stating: 'The auditor's function is also to be seen in terms of social control.' Mackenzie, in the foreword to *The Accountability and Audit of Governments* makes a similar point: 'Without audit, no accountability; without accountability, no control; and if there is no control, where is the seat of power?' (Normanton, 1966, p. vii). Tricker (1982, p. 58) argues that 'auditing can only be studied in a socio-political context and that the study of auditing needs a supportive theory of corporate regulation and the exercise of social power and prerogative . . . such a theory would identify the place and purpose of the audit function in the model of corporate regulation.'

It is certainly true that as a matter of fact almost universally where there is an audit of any description there is a relationship in which one party owes a duty of accountability of some kind to another or others. The parties may be individuals or groups or classes of individuals. There are, however, many situations in which an audit is not called for, although there is a duty of accountability in which one of the parties wants to be informed as to the performance of the other who is accountable. There are also areas in which a duty of accountability has existed in the past where an audit has not been required, and where the extension of the audit function is now being canvassed. Social accountability of business and other organisations, for example, is not a new concept, but the idea of a social audit is. The demand for more extensive scrutiny of economy, efficiency and effectiveness, not only in public administration but also in business, illustrates the evolving nature of the criteria by which accountability has to be demonstrated.

So there must be circumstances other than accountability alone which occasion the invocation of the audit process. The presence of a duty of accountability is an important circumstance, possibly the most important circumstance, but there are others which need to be identified. It appears from the current debate and from the changes which are being canvassed that audit is an evolving process, reacting with changing expectations about the performance or conduct of the individuals or organisations to which it is applied. In so far as the audit process is designed to monitor compliance with specified norms of what is acceptable behaviour, it is clearly culturally, socially and politically dependent.

The standards of acceptable behaviour must derive from the value system and the mores and sanctions of the total environment of the society. Accordingly, while the principles of audit may be universally applicable throughout the world, the particular applications, the specific standards of expected performance and the recognised audit practices are unlikely to show the same uniformity, although they should be consistent with the culture of the particular society. A different history, a different set of traditions, a different culture, a different course of economic development, a different set of national characteristics, and so on, have resulted, it is suggested, in different corporate structures, regulatory mechanisms, institutions and business environment in, for example, West Germany, the USA and the United Kingdom. The Special Committee of the Canadian Institute of Chartered Accountants (CICA) (1978, para. A10), set up to examine the role of the auditor, wrote: 'Our perception of the differences between the US and Canadian environments has, in many cases, been an important factor in determining whether we consider certain developments in the US relevant to the Canadian scene.' The cultural dependence of audit means also that even in any one society, while the concept may remain constant, the practice of the function will change in sympathy and harmony with other changes in that society.

Honesty and regularity as basic standards of accountability presuppose a social philosophy which places prime importance on ethical precepts and legal principles and rules as measures of acceptable behaviour. Without derogating from these standards as first principles of accountability in business, public administration or any form of social organisation, expectations of performance can be enlarged for economic, political or sociological reasons to seek, for example, efficiency, effectiveness, protection of the environment, or conservation of energy as primary objectives. In industry and commerce, profit as a measure of efficient stewardship can be supplemented by less easily quantifiable standards such as, for example, service to customers, maintenance of employment, or cost effectiveness. In public administration, economy and efficiency of operations may be more easily measured but are not more important than effectiveness in achieving social policy objectives as criteria of accountability. In terms of public policy, for example, energy conservation may be more important than minimising short-term costs.

Accountability is not a simple concept. It is one which requires to be defined, and its definition needs to have regard to the fact that social attitudes and expectations do change. In addition, the parties who are entitled to expect or exact accountability do not necessarily remain constant. Interpretation of the requirements of audit will therefore depend on the obligations of accountability in each case.

Audit as a social phenomenon

A simple definition of audit is that it is an examination: but it is a particular kind of examination. A proper understanding of its meaning requires an appreciation of its dynamic function in society. Audit is a social phenomenon. It has no purpose or value except in its practical usefulness. It is wholly utilitarian. The function has evolved in response to a perceived need of individuals or groups in society who seek information or reassurance about the conduct or performance of others in which they have an acknowledged and legitimate interest: it exists because the interested individuals or groups are unable for one or more reasons to obtain for themselves the information or reassurance they require.

The social concept of audit is a special kind of examination by a person other than the parties involved which compares performance with expectation and reports the result: it is part of the public and private control mechanism of monitoring and securing accountability.

Audit's foundation in social need is a crucially important characteristic. In a changing and developing society the interpretation of the practical implementations of the audit concept must be the result of a constant interaction between the relevant groups and the auditors. Auditors must be sensitive to the changing expectations of the relevant groups while at the same time containing these expectations within the constraints of what is possible. There are inevitably economic and practical limitations on what an audit can do, and this is something which those who wish the benefit of audit must understand.

The social machinery for interaction between auditors and audit policy-makers and the relevant interest groups is informal and unstructured, but it is important that it should be effective. A failure on the part of auditors or audit policy-makers to recognise the dynamic nature of auditing or to respond to legitimate societal pressure will result in frustration of the social purpose and the emergence of the kind of 'expectation gap' and misunderstanding to which reference has been made.

While it is necessary to have clearly understood terms of reference and well-defined lines of responsibility, a too rigid perception of an audit purpose in terms of criteria of performance or of interested parties, and the reluctance or resistance to change on the part of auditors or audit policy-makers, will inhibit progress and development in a changing society. There is an understandable caution on the part of auditors voluntarily to assume new responsibilities which may be imperfectly defined when the penalties − in terms of personal financial liability in damages − are severe: it is necessary, therefore, to create a system whereby the relevant interest groups can secure the reassurance and protection they desire without exposing the auditors to unreasonable and unsupportable risks.

In the private sector business corporations have had, as a matter of history, a primary duty of accountability to members or shareholders (providers of capital), and the audit responsibility has been conceived and defined in law to monitor that duty. But as corporations have grown in size, importance and influence – socially, economically and politically – and as social structures and public expectations have changed, there has emerged an expectation that the duty of accountability is wider in its scope and more varied in its terms. The state has a concern to protect the public interest; employee groups have an interest in continuing and expanding employment opportunities; shareholders or members may no longer be an effective group to exercise the function of 'owners'; in international groups a number of governments have different and perhaps conflicting concerns; and there is some duty of accountability to all of these. Auditors who see the corporation or company and its members as their only 'client' and resist moves to recognise other representative bodies, such as regulatory or supervisory agencies with a concern for the public interest, or employee groups, as legitimately entitled to be directly addressed by the auditors, understand neither the nature of the concept of accountability nor the social function of the audit.

Social determination of the auditors' role

In a paper on 'The Role of the Independent Auditor in a Market Economy' prepared for the AICPA Commission on Auditors' Responsibilities, Mautz (1975a) writes that the role of the independent auditor in a market economy is resolved ultimately by social consent:

> **society either accepts or rejects the role that a professional group assumes for itself; in time the group either finds a role acceptable to society or the group disappears. As conditions and apparent needs change, society may reject roles formerly considered acceptable so professional groups must continually be alert to the desirability of role modification and revision.** (Mautz, 1975a, p. 2)

Recognising that there are few people in society who are well enough informed to vote intelligently on such a technical and complex issue as the appropriate role for a professional group,

Mautz concludes that independent auditors must 'select for themselves what appears to be a reasonable role and set out both to fulfil it and to convince others of its propriety in the circumstances. If they are unsuccessful in either effect, they must modify their activity until they do discover a role which society accepts and which they can perform.' He adds the warning that:

> **technically competent minorities should strive to lead, not merely follow, the majority. To do so, they must recognise an obligation of convincing others of the reasonableness of their proposed leadership. If there ever was a time when society readily followed those who claimed expert knowledge, that time seems to have passed. The consumer emphasis in our present society requires every producer not only to meet the market demand for an acceptable product at an acceptable price but also to be prepared to justify the social desirability of both.** (Mautz, 1975a, p. 3)

The underlying philosophy of the theoretical approach of this text follows these propositions. Audit is a social control mechanism for securing accountability. The onus is on auditors and audit policy-makers constantly to seek to find out what is the societal need and expectation for independent audit and to endeavour to fulfil that need within the limits of practical and economic constraints, remembering at all times that the function is a dynamic, not a static one.

Basic Postulates 2

2.1 Introduction

Audit has been an evolving function in all sectors of developed societies, particularly over the last hundred or so years. Although there are inevitable limitations, already acknowledged, imposed by the bias of the cultural, institutional and regulatory environment in any one country, general principles can be deduced to provide a basis for the development of a theory of general application.

Historically, auditing has been concerned for centuries with the honest and accurate accounting for money and property in the affairs of state, in the services of central and local government and other public bodies, in the business affairs of the early merchants, landowners, merchant adventurers, manufacturers and persons engaged in every form of commercial and industrial undertaking, and in the transactions of other institutions and organisations large and small. Stewardship and accountability for the custody of money and other resources, for their management in husbandry, estate management, trade, manufacture, provision of services, and other activities, and for their application to designated purposes, have been duties of which the discharge by the persons responsible has been the subject of audit.

In its origins the purpose of the audit was to find out if these duties had been carried out honestly, with propriety and with regularity (in accordance with law and specific instructions). As time has passed the concept of accountability in the sense of honesty, propriety and regularity has enlarged as new standards of performance have evolved from the expectations of the interested groups: specialised applications such as operational auditing and management auditing have been developed, and new criteria of performance have been introduced to supplement honesty, propriety and regularity as measures of accountability. The scope of accountability has expanded to include more than the management of resources. The underlying philosophy has, however, been constant: the purpose of the audit is to investigate and review the actions (or inaction), decisions, achievements, statements or reports of specified persons with defined responsibilities, to compare these actions, etc. with some norm, and to form and express an opinion on the result of that investigation, review and comparison.

2.2 The Postulates

A starting point for the development of a structure of audit theory and knowledge of the audit phenomenon is to observe this evolution and to make some *a priori* hypotheses about the nature of auditing from the evidence that is available of societal expectations and current audit functions. The propositions which follow are put forward as the postulates of auditing on the basis that they incorporate fundamental principles on which a theory of auditing can be constructed. They are proposed as postulates in the sense of indemonstrable principles.[1] They are hypotheses about auditing, the truth, validity and consistency of which will be tested by logical deduction in the development of the theoretical structure. In due course the validity of the propositions which are confirmed by logical deduction should be capable of being demonstrated by empirical evidence.

While the primary purpose of the postulates is to establish a basis for theory development, they also describe the intrinsic characteristics of audit and define a model with which potential audit situations may be compared. Satisfying the relevant conditions of the basic postulates does not necessarily mean than an audit will take place. It may only mean that an audit could take place if it is required: it may mean, in the case of a situation of public accountability, that in the public interest an audit should take place. Satisfying some but not all the relevant conditions is unlikely to be sufficient to enable an audit to be carried out, even if there is a public or private demand for some duty of accountability to be monitored by audit. This particular type of examination – an audit – is not always possible, even if it is desired, because of an inability to satisfy one or more of the conditions. The existence of a situation of accountability (postulate 1), for example, does not necessarily mean that an audit can be carried out, however important it may be thought to be, if relevant criteria have not been established and agreed by reference to which performance can be judged (postulate 5). A useful investigation and report can be carried out, but it should not be described as an audit.

In practical terms there are degrees of materiality in judging the importance of any one postulate in particular situations, but as a general rule if the status, authority and public reputation of 'audit' are to be preserved, a rigorous application of the postulates is highly desirable. Examination of current practice and writing shows, for example, that on some occasions there is confused thinking and a failure to distinguish between a management audit and management consultancy. Valuable as a social audit may be, there may be some reservations at the present stage of development about its status as an 'audit' when the investigation and report are judged against the conditions of the seven postulates.

These illustrations, however, only point to the importance of developing definitive criteria for an 'audit' if its present undoubted value as a high-quality instrument of social control is not to become debased by use of the term to describe examinations and reports which, because of their inherent character, cannot have the peculiar independent and other qualities which distinguish an audit.

The following basic postulates are, therefore, proposed on those premises as a definitive framework and foundation for the construction of a theory of auditing and the formulation of principles of practice.

1. The primary condition for an audit is that there is either:

    (a) a relationship of accountability between two or more

parties in the sense that there is a duty of acceptable conduct or performance owed by one party to the other party or parties;

(b) a need by some party to establish the reliability and credibility of information for which they are responsible which is expected to be used and relied on by a specified group or groups of which the members may not be constant or individually identifiable, producing constructively a relationship of accountability;

(c) a public interest dimension to the quality of the conduct or performance of some party, resulting in a situation of public accountability; or

(d) a need or a desire to establish the authenticity of information given or statements made by some party which are intended to or are likely to influence the actions of unspecified members of the general public or a section of it, producing constructively a situation of public accountability.

2. The subject matter of accountability is too remote, too complex and/or of too great significance for the discharge of the duty to be demonstrated without the process of audit.

3. Essential distinguishing characteristics of audit are the independence of its status and its freedom from investigatory and reporting constraints.

4. The subject matter of audit, for example conduct, performance or achievement, or record of events or state of affairs, or a statement or facts relating to any of these, is susceptible to verification by evidence.

5. Standards of accountability, for example of conduct, performance, achievement and quality of information, can be set for those who are accountable; actual conduct, performance, achievement, quality and so on can be measured and compared with those standards by reference to known criteria; and the process of measurement and comparison requires special skill and the exercise of judgement.

6. The meaning, significance and intention of financial and other statements and data which are audited are sufficiently clear that the credibility which is given thereto as a result of audit can be clearly expressed and communicated.

7. An audit produces an economic or social benefit.

1. The primary condition for an audit is that there is a relationship of accountability or a situation of public accountability.

While audit is an integral part of the process of accountability, and accordingly the existence of a requirement of accountability must be a primary condition of audit, some elaboration is necessary for the postulate to be better understood. Accountability is a complex concept, and in the context of audit different situations can be distinguished.

There is the familiar situation of postulate 1(a) above in which the two parties can be specifically identified and the relationship between them is direct. Directors of a company are accountable to the members or shareholders: the elected committee and appointed officials of an association, society or club are accountable to the members of the organisation. In the case of government the situation is similar, but not identical. Appointed officials are accountable in the first instance to the elected members of government, who in turn are accountable to the electorate. The appointed officials are indirectly accountable to the electorate, but the elected members are responsible for securing their accountability. The elected members, too, are likely to have a multiple duty of accountability, not only to the electorate but also, depending on the level of government and the constitutional arrangements, to superior levels of government or to international agencies. For example, local, district, regional or provincial governments may derive resources from, or in respect of certain functions be the agent of, central government, and owe a duty of accountability in these respects. There is also, as will be referred to below, a duty of public accountability in relation to government services, and the government owes specific duties to members of the community at large according to their interest, whether or not they are electors.

There are clearly recognisable lines of responsibility between the parties in these cases and a duty for one party to perform, to be held accountable for their performance, and to give an account of that performance. The account is likely to include a statement in financial terms, but considered conceptually there is no reason why it should be limited to this. What has to be considered are the criteria by which the interested groups can best judge whether the duty has been satisfactorily discharged.

The essential element is that the actions of the first party in all these cases are subject to scrutiny by another group or groups who are in a position to invoke or impose some sanction or penalty if the performance falls short of what can be expected by reference to the criteria that have been established. The first parties require to give an account, provide information or provide access to information as a basis of decision by the group or groups to whom they are accountable.

The case of postulate 1(b) is where some party produces an account or information which is publicly available and which is known to be likely to be used and to be relied on in connection with action affecting that party by an identifiable group or groups, the individual membership of which may not be constant and may not be known, and with which the first party does not necessarily have a continuing direct relationship. The quality of the account or information is important to the users, and the first party's knowledge of this produces constructively a relationship of accountability which may not be legally constituted but which is real in practical terms. Such a case would be the use of company accounts by lenders, suppliers, prospective investors, investment advisers, and employees and their representatives. The importance to the first party of establishing the reliability and credibility of the account or information creates a situation which is a primary condition for an adult.

Governments, public bodies, international agencies, charitable foundations and similar organisations, some of which have no immediate constituency to which they are accountable, have a public responsibility for the way in which they discharge some or all of their functions. Particularly in respect of the resources which are provided to them for the discharge of their functions, irrespective of the source of these resources – taxes, loans, grants, levies, subscriptions, donations, etc. – they have an obligation to ensure that they are applied only for the purposes for which they were provided, that they are applied effectively, and that they are administered efficiently. The duty of accountability is a public one creating a situation which is a primary condition for an audit.

This situation could also apply in the case of individuals or groups of individuals who are engaged independently in carrying out a public function mainly in the provision of a professional service. There is a duty of accountability for efficiency and effectiveness with which the service is provided which satisfies the primary condition. An illustration of this might be medical audit, which is concerned with a review of the quality of medical care by reference to some stated criteria.[2]

Finally, there is the rather exceptional case of postulate 1(d) above, where the public release of information imposes a duty of public accountability. There is no formal accountability and the public could be free to ignore the information. The fact that the publisher of the information wants the public to accept it, and the potential for misinformation damaging to the public interest because of the apparent authority derived from the status of the publisher, create the duty and also a situation which satisfies the primary condition. Whether the conditions of the other postulates can be satisfied will be a matter for consideration in each case. The kind of situation which is covered by this case is the publication of circulation figures by a newspaper. This is done presumably to impress present and potential readers, but the value of such information is limited unless it has been subject to independent verification, i.e. the accountability has been demonstrated. (Information for advertisers and prospective advertisers need not be public, although it would certainly need to be certified.)

It is perhaps debatable whether this is a true audit situation. Attestation of quantitative or non-quantitative information or statements against stated criteria in individual situations is not necessarily an audit. Authoritative attestation is a useful function in society requiring the professional skills and qualities normally associated with an auditor. As a result the authority of an auditor may be drawn on for attestation or certification in these situations. According to the concept of audit which has been proposed, these activities are not by this fact alone considered to be audits. To include all of them would result in an extension of the concept of audit. There must inevitably be some uncertainty at the margin, but a rigorous application of the postulates is highly desirable.

2. The subject matter of accountability is too remote, too complex and/or of too great significance for the discharge of the duty to be demonstrated without the process of audit.

This proposition recognises the fact there are situations as defined in the first postulate which do not need to rely on audit to secure accountability or to inform the interested parties on how the duty has been discharged. It identifies the peculiar features of a situation of accountability which result in an audit being required. It explains why issues of accountability which had previously not been subject to audit are perceived by society as needing to be brought within its scope.

There are situations in which the interested parties have the capacity to inform themselves on all or some aspects of accountability; there are situations in which the criteria of acceptability are so personal or subjective that only the interested parties can satisfy themselves; and there are situations in which the interested parties are prepared to rely on the information which they have in an unaudited state. The proposition of the postulate is that it is remoteness, complexity and significance which are the circumstances that dictate that audit is a necessary part of securing accountability. There are, of course, degrees of remoteness, complexity and significance, and the greater these are the more important it will be for securing accountability that an audit is carried out.

In this connection remoteness means that there are barriers to access by the interested parties to the means of satisfying themselves on the matter of accountability. It is not only a question of geographical separation from the source of data, such as would affect dispersed shareholders of a company or electors of a government. There may be legal, organisational, time or cost difficulties in the way of individual parties taking their own steps to access the source data.

Even if these difficulties did not exist, the complexity of the operations for which accountability is due and, in appropriate cases, the recording of them, are such that the specialised knowledge and scale of resources that are necessary to investigate them are beyond the personal capacity of most interested parties without specialist assistance. To have this replicated for all interested parties would be intolerable for the persons audited and a thoroughly wasteful and uneconomic use of resources.

In the earliest days of corporate business enterprises, it was believed that the conduct and performance of directors could be judged by their honesty, conformity to law and the regulations of the enterprise, and the quantum of profits and dividends. As compared to the previous unincorporated partnership or joint venture situation, an audit became necessary because of the separation between the directors and the other interested parties, including not only the providers of shareholders' capital but also lenders and suppliers at risk with the introduction of limited liability. In the intervening period of more than one hundred years, business, corporate structures and the duties of directors have become more complex, the capital market has become more sophisticated, the composition of the shareholding group has not only grown but changed with the development of investment trusts, finance companies, insurance funds, pension funds and similar organisations, the rights and interests of other stakeholders have become formally or informally recognised, and there has been a revolution in social thinking as regards the responsibilities of corporate business. As a consequence, the concept of accountability has become more complex and has resulted in an enhanced expectation of the audit.

Similarly, the extension of the scope of the functions of government at all levels, the scale of the resources that are administered, and the highly specialised nature of the services have not only placed new emphasis on the importance of audit in securing accountability but have also required and stimulated the development of new criteria for judging the quality of performance.

Finally, the way in which public and private organisations discharge their duty of accountability is important in greater or lesser degree not only for its effect on their own constituencies but also for its impact on the wider community. As the performance of an organisation and the information it gives about that performance increase in importance to its immediate interested parties – for example, shareholders or electors – so also does the significance of any deficiency or inadequacy, and an audit to monitor the performance and verify the information becomes increasingly necessary. 'Significance' in this connection means the relative importance of the performance and/or the information to the judgement and decisions of the interested parties. The quality of company accounts and the extent of information disclosed, for example, are vital for any rational judgement on management performance, company prospects, and investing, lending or credit decisions. The accounts also constitute part of the information required for assessment to taxation, judging social performance and formulating wage claims. The significance of the information is such that it is essential to establish its reliability and credibility without reservation and with independent authority.

The validity of the postulate can also be illustrated by the way in which the state has used the audit as an instrument of social control in those organisations which are perceived as having some public accountability or in which it is seen to be necessary to prescribe a minimum standard of private accountability in the public interest. Incorporated companies, banks, building societies, regional and district governments, public utilities, public boards and other similar organisations are required, with progressively greater detailed specification as the remoteness, complexity and significance have increased, not only to produce annual accounts and to publish them but also to have them audited. It is perhaps curious that an annual accounting attested by audit has not yet been required by law of all unincorporated organisations, except only, perhaps, for the very small. The trend of opinion is to require of *all* organisations in society not only a greater degree of accountability but a public manifestation of that accountability. It is at least partly because of the increasing complexity and significance of social intercourse and relationships that the conduct of unincorporated organisations is seen to be a matter not solely of private but also of public concern. Prescribed standards of accountability and mandatory audit are almost inevitable consequences.

3. Essential distinguishing characteristics of audit are the independence of its status and its freedom from investigatory and reporting constraints.

The societal expectation in relation to audit and the circumstances in which the audit phenomenon has appeared, demonstrate without qualification that a definitive characteristic of the audit process is that it should be independent in every sense from the organisation and the members of the organisation who are subject to audit. This means that the audit view that is taken or the audit judgement that is formed should be completely objective, unprejudiced by previous involvement in the subject of audit, uncompromised by vested interest in the outcome or its consequences, unbiased and uninfluenced by considerations extraneous to the matter at issue. It is primarily on the basis of its independence that the audit derives its authority and its acceptance. In all the situations in which the audit process is applied, the parties who have a duty of accountability have accepted the obligations of those duties, for example to conduct themselves, to perform or to report by reference to agreed standards and criteria. Their actions, achievements and reports convey information on how they have met these obligations. They are in a position to control or to influence the content of that information by which they are to be judged. They have a vested interest in the substance and quality of that information. Even the most fair-minded are understandably likely to be unable to take a dispassionate view of how their own actions and achievements should be reported and judged. There are others who for their own reasons would wish to colour the perception of outsiders of what they had done. The purpose of the audit is to secure accountability. It is essential that the audit should be able to disarm the public's natural scepticism about the impartiality of information prepared by the accountable on their own accountability. To secure accountability and reassure the relevant public the audit must be completely independent of those whose conduct, etc. is being monitored. If the audit were under their influence or control to any extent it would inevitably add little, and at the extreme would add nothing to knowledge of or confidence in the standard of their accountability.

The objective of the audit is a skilled and informed audit report and opinion on matters of importance and complexity, passing judgement on what the persons responsible have already achieved. To enable this to be done with the competence and authority necessary to fulfil its social purpose, the conduct of the audit and the access to information must be at least equal to that of those who are audited and be free from direction and constraint. On completion of the audit the opinion and report must be freely available to those who are entitled to receive it – and in some cases this may mean publication.

Any limitation on the freedom of investigation and pursuit of evidence, or restriction on the freedom of reporting, would inevitably result in a reservation in the audit opinion and report, would be damaging to the authority of the audit, and would frustrate the social purpose.

These propositions are well illustrated in practice. Independence is a cardinal principle of state audit; it must be free of direction and control by government. Normanton (1966, p. 298) explains the principle, recounting that 'Since the time of Aristotle it has been accepted principle that state auditors should be free from direction, influence and intimidation by, and income or reward from, the authorities and persons whose affairs they are called upon to audit'. He emphasises the issue in these terms: 'No state auditor, or at any rate no chief state auditor, can afford to be without independence; he needs it as a judge needs it, in order to be impartial and fearless in criticism. He also needs it in order to be able to publicise his criticism in an open report.' In the case of a company, the directors have a statutory duty to present accounts which give a true and fair view of results and state of affairs and are in breach of their duty if they fail to do so. The authority and value of the audit derive entirely from the fact that the auditors, in expressing an opinion on that view, do so independently. If the auditors were not independent, that opinion would add little or nothing. An internal audit by reason of being internal is limited in its independence, being subject to direction and control within the organisation. But within the limitations of its scope it must be independent, unconnected with the execution of those matters which are subject to examination, review and appraisal.

The concept of audit independence as a source of audit authority is so central to the meaning of the audit concept itself that it constitutes a separate element in the theoretical structure.

It is essential to understand what constitutes and supports independence, what it implies in terms of personal qualities and qualifications of the auditor, what it requires in terms of constitutional and organisational arrangements, and what is necessary to create and sustain public confidence in its existence. Without these there cannot be an audit.

4. The subject matter of audit, for example conduct, performance or achievement or record of events or state of affairs, or a statement or facts relating to any of these, is susceptible to verification by evidence.

Audit is part of the process of securing accountability. It is an examination by a person other than those involved to find out and to report on how the duty of accountability has been discharged. It is an investigatory process, an *ex-post* examination of the matter under scrutiny. What is sought of an audit is a skilled, informed opinion.

Audit involves investigation, examination, consideration, appraisal and evaluation of conduct, performance, achievement, events, state of affairs or statements generally for periods or at a date which are past. Audit may, however, also be concerned with future projections of these. While there are other benefits obtained from an audit, the principal benefit is the report and opinion of the auditors as a result of that investigation.

The only way in which auditors can inform themselves on the matters on which they must report and express an opinion is by obtaining evidence which relates to these matters. Without evidence auditors have no basis on which to form a judgement and express an opinion. If there is no evidence an audit is not possible. If the matters which it is proposed should be audited are not susceptible to verification by evidence – for example, they are wholly subjective and matters of opinion without external independent sources of authentication – an audit is not possible.

The nature, quality and persuasive effect of evidence will vary. It comes from a number of sources bearing on the matter which is the subject of audit. Audit evidence includes oral evidence (responses to enquiries), written evidence (documents and formal and informal writings of all descriptions), physical productions, and the product of systematic reasoning based on judgemental and statistical inference and probability (for example, from examination of a system of accounting and internal control or analytical review of financial performance).

The evidence that is necessary to support an opinion depends on the terms of that opinion which are derived from the auditors' terms of reference, i.e. the nature of the audit responsibility.

It is a matter of personal skill for auditors to judge how much, what kind, and what combination of different types of evidence are necessary to enable an opinion justifiably to be formed and a report to be made. There must be what Mautz and Sharaf (1961, pp. 43, 68) describe as sufficient 'competent evidential matter'. 'Verification', they say, 'is the vehicle that carries one to a position of confidence about any given proposition'.

The theory of audit evidence is at the core of audit theory. Development of a theoretical framework requires an identification and analysis of the characteristics of audit evidence and an interpretation of probability theory and statistical inference in relation to the persuasive value of different types of audit evidence. It is only on such a basis that it is possible to formulate audit practices and procedures and to test their validity.

5. Standards of accountability, for example of conduct, performance, achievement and quality of information, can be set for those who are accountable; actual conduct, performance, achievement, quality and so on can be measured and compared with these standards by reference to known criteria; and the process of measurement and comparison requires special skill and the exercise of judgement.

This proposition states a demanding definitive characteristic of audit which distinguishes it from other examinations or investigations which may be directed to aspects of accountability or to other situations under review.

It is implicit in the concept of accountability that the two or more parties in the situation have some perception of the standards of conduct, performance or achievement, of information or of the kind of report that are required. The party who is responsible for the activity and who has the duty of accountability should know what standards are expected in respect of that particular duty. The parties to whom the duty of accountability is owed have an expectation in relation to these standards. It is important that the standards should be clearly established and the perceptions of the two parties should coincide.

If the parties were in direct communication, any differences of opinion could be resolved and the parties to whom the accountability is due could exercise their own subjective judgement as to whether the conduct, performance and account were acceptable. In the audit situation, however, the duty and the expectation must be clearly specified. Auditors require to have agreed criteria against which to compare conduct, performance, information or account.

If auditors were to set their own standards on each occasion for each organisation, carry out an investigation and report their findings, this might well be interesting and valuable. It would be likely, however, to fail to satisfy any of the interested parties. The persons audited could reject it as irrelevant to their interpretation of their duty. The persons for whom the audit is carried out could reject it as not conforming to their expectations. The general utility of it would be minimal, since there would be no uniformity between similar organisations, and users would require to inform themselves on the basis of the audit in each case.

If it is not possible to specify the standard of conduct, performance, achievement and quality of information in the relevant report or account in terms which are understandable to and acceptable to all parties, there is no basis on which to instruct an audit. Audit as a concept has a universal meaning: but the operational interpretation of audit is specific to the particular definition of accountability.

It is essential to know what are the principal measures of accountability: honesty, regularity and legality, profitability, economy, efficiency, effectiveness or some other factor? A simple statement of any of these is not sufficient: specific criteria are required.

A duty of honesty appears clear enough, but even in this case clarification is required. Honesty within the organisation is required; so also is honesty between the organisation, its directors and managers on one hand and its members or 'relevant constituency in society' on the other. But what precisely does this mean? In addition, since those who are directing, managing or administering the organisation also have responsibilities, at what level in the organisation do auditors' responsibilities begin and end? The attitude of members of society to relationships between an organisation and other parties with which it deals sometimes appears uncertain, confused or ambivalent. How 'honest' are 'facilitating payments', or 'questionable payments'? Are 'bribes' or questionable payments or illegal payments objectionable if they are incurred for the benefit of the organisation?

Public debate on this and similar issues reveals an uncertain situation and leaves auditors in an unsatisfactory position. The auditors' personal standards of truth, honesty and integrity must be absolute. Auditors must recognise these doubtful transactions for what they are, but for each particular audit what and to whom is it the auditors' duty to report? The auditors' duty is to specified persons or classes of persons, and in general auditors do not have any open-ended responsibility to the public for standards of morality or law enforcement.

The criteria of honesty are not without difficulty, but establishing objective measures of, for example, economy, efficiency, effectiveness, value for money, waste and extravagance can present even greater problems. What are the objective criteria for judging maladministration? It may not be too difficult to decide if accounts comply with the requirements of the law if the law is sufficiently detailed and specific, but other standards for reporting are less clear cut: for example, the concept of 'fairness' in reporting or of 'a true and fair view' in accounts is not well defined, but must be agreed to be susceptible to sufficiently universal understanding to be operationally viable.[3] Elaboration of the terms to read 'present fairly *in accordance with generally accepted accounting principles*' only changes the problem, but does not solve it when 'principles', 'acceptance', and 'fairly' can be argued to be matters of subjective opinion.

These are all standards of conduct, performance or reporting which are widely applied in public administration, government, commerce and industry. If actual conduct, etc. is to be compared with what is expected, with the prospect that some consequence will flow from the report on that comparison and perhaps some sanction imposed if the conduct, etc. falls short by too great a margin as disclosed by audit, it is imperative that the criteria for these standards have been established, that there is a consensus among the parties as to what they are, and that they can be communicated to the auditors.

Audit is a part of a control mechanism. In some applications it is part of the machinery of social control. Control is by its nature a restraint on freedom, and accordingly the terms and limitations of the audit restraint must be agreed and specified. Otherwise, there may be an undue restraint which is inhibiting to effective action and acceptance of responsibility: alternatively, there may be ineffectual control.

The major issue is, however, that auditors must have clear and specific terms of reference which are constant for a continuing audit engagement and consistent with audit engagements of the same class and which are capable of objective specific prescription. Otherwise, an audit which meets the conceptual model which is represented here is not possible. The social objective of an audit can be achieved only if standards of accountability are established for each class of organisation and each type of audit.

As already indicated, there is particular difficulty in specifying criteria of, for example, economy, efficiency, effectiveness or profitability. Other measures of accountability may produce even greater problems. Every organisation has a number of conflicting goals or objectives, competing demands for resources, and long and short timescales for measuring success or achievement.

Directors, managers, administrators – or other appropriate decision-takers in each organisation – must act within their knowledge and competence in conditions of uncertainty, whereas audit generally takes place with the benefit of hindsight when results have been achieved and many earlier uncertainties resolved. Auditors have to consider whether the decision or action taken or the arrangements made were satisfactory in the conditions and with the available knowledge at the time. Leaving aside this particular practical difficulty, the theoretical problem is how to devise definitive criteria for standards which are substantially subjective. If perfection were the standard, then in conditions of uncertainty conduct or performance would inevitably almost always fall short. If, for example, maximum profit were the standard, what would be the timescale over which this was to be judged, and what constraints would have to be relaxed in order to achieve it – regard for conditions of work, terms of employment, protection of the environment, avoidance of pollution?

Economy, efficiency and effectiveness, particularly in government and public administration, are very much dependent on or constrained by matters of policy and politics. Policy review is a separate activity from audit of economy and efficiency, so that an auditor requires to separate the diseconomies and the inefficiencies implicit in a policy decision from those incurred in actually carrying it out. Evaluation of effectiveness requires that the objectives of policy are stated in terms which can be quantified or specified so that the results can be expressed in the same terms for the purposes of comparison. Especially in government and public administration, this is a matter of particular difficulty.

While economy, efficiency and effectiveness need to be considered in the context of a given policy, there are circumstances in which policy-making itself will come under audit scrutiny. This is so in a management audit, where the goals of the organisation have been established and the policies being pursued to achieve them are subject to scrutiny. Political policy decisions are not susceptible to audit: accountability for these is to the electorate, who make their own judgements.

An examination of such measures of performance as economy, efficiency and effectiveness which is not based on established criteria is not an audit.

Management audit and operational audit clearly present difficulties. The subject matters of audit are diverse and their susceptibility to objective measurement is variable. In an operational audit, which is directed to providing a measure of the achievement of an organisation towards its goals and objectives, the organisation provides the overriding criteria for measurement in the definition of goals and objectives, although when this is broken down into its several functional parts the issues are likely to be more complex. It is essential that throughout the organisation duties, responsibilities and objectives should be clearly specified.

Management audit encompasses scrutiny of managerial objectives, plans and strategies and the effectiveness of management in performance of its responsibilities. For such an audit to be possible by reference to objective independent criteria there require to be professional standards for the different fuñctional areas of an organisation and for different types and sizes of organisation. There is certainly a societal expectation for such an application of the audit concept, and an integral part of that expectation is that there are definitive standards to which management should conform. If the definitive standards of management in any one organisation, or class or group of organisation, are not explicitly specified in detail, the legitimacy of the audit, in the sense of its credibility and acceptance, is dependent on the interpretation of the expectation and the standard by the auditors as seems appropriate in the circumstances by reference to some overriding criteria within an agreed and understood framework. This means that auditors must specify and justify the criteria that have been used with an authority which is acknowledged by all parties. Without such a framework and overriding criteria, and in the absence of acceptance of the auditors' authority, the social utility of such an examination is likely to be minimal.

In the case of social audit the societal expectation is that the audit process should be applied to a wider concept of social accountability. It has to be considered, however, whether the situation has been reached when the broad framework within which the detailed criteria for measuring performance are to be determined has been agreed. The concepts of social responsibility are still too general and lacking in definitive characteristics to make the conduct of organisations auditable against known standards by reference to known criteria. The gap between the frame of reference and the area for the exercise of judgement is too wide for an 'auditor' to bridge. This may be an evolutionary difficulty. It is not intended to undervalue or criticise the work that is done in the name of social audit. It is suggested that it has not yet evolved to a stage when it can properly claim to be an audit according to the definition which is being used. It is accordingly a useful illustration to reinforce the significance of this fifth basic postulate.

In all the audit situations which have been cited the criteria of measurement lack specification to a lesser or greater degree. Even where satisfactory standards of accountability have been set and the criteria of comparison of actual with expectation are well established and understood, the audit is not a straightforward process of inspection and checking. Understanding the complexity and subjectivity of the subject matter, and evaluation of the discharge of the duty of accountability are not simple and automatic, but responsible and difficult tasks requiring special skills and a capacity for the exercise of judgement. This independent professional nature of the process is one of the distinguishing characteristics of audit.

Complexity of the issues is one of the features of audit. Auditors can be capable of exercising judgement, and that judgement will be accepted by the parties as having authority only if the auditors are possessed of appropriate special knowledge, skill and experience in the relevant fields, for example of public administration, general management, accounting and finance.

6. *The meaning, significance and intention of financial and other statements and data which are audited are sufficiently clear that the credibility which is given thereto as a result of audit can be clearly expressed and communicated.*

Statements and data which are subjected to audit have an information value in their unaudited state. The purpose of the audit is to add to that information value by expressing an opinion on the credibility, meaning, significance, reliability, legitimacy, legality or regularity of the statement or the data. The audit lends some authority, or alternatively explicitly denies authority, to the message which the originator of the statement or the data intended to convey. Accordingly, if the message of the originator is confused, ambiguous or uncertain, it is not susceptible to audit. The intention of the information or the data must be clarified before it can be audited. In turn, the significance of the audit attestation must also be clear, specific and unambiguous so that those parties who use it will be able to understand in what respect the quality of the information or data has been changed as a result of audit.

The terms of an auditors' report or opinion are a crucial part of an audit. There may be behavioural and other benefits from an audit, but the principal advantage is derived from a communication by the auditors which is intended to produce a response in those who read it and who have a legitimate interest in its subject matter.

If auditors fail to communicate effectively, the audit purpose is frustrated. If, for example, an unincorporated business organisation, which has no constitutional document regulating the preparation of accounts, presents accounts without any statement of objectives or accounting policies, the basis on which they are prepared is uncertain. If the auditors were then to docket them as 'audited and found correct', any other party relying on these accounts would do so at their peril. Both the accounts and the audit report are inadequate. It is, of course, possible for auditors to impute a clear intention to statements or data which are confused or ambiguous and, with an explicit preamble of assumptions, to lend authority to the interpretation which has been imputed. An audit, however, cannot proceed except on the basis that the meaning, significance and intention of statements and data which are to be audited are clear.

7. *An audit produces an economic or social benefit.*

This postulate emphasises a cost-benefit test as a social justification for auditing. Audit is a wholly utilitarian function, and it only satisfies the social need if the benefit it provides is greater than the sacrifice made to obtain it. The implication of the proposition is, for example, that financial and other statements and data which are audited must have an added utility which more than matches the cost. The audit benefit is frequently intangible. Attempts to measure it have so far been unsuccessful.[4] The audit process is not under the control of either party, since to impose such a control would infringe the audit independence. Society is therefore dependent on auditors to produce the benefit at the minimum social cost. The economic cost can be seen by society; the benefit has to be assessed subjectively.

In all audits, but particularly in the audit of financial and other statements and data, obtaining and evaluating sufficient evidence to support the propositions or assertions being audited is a substantial part of the work. Auditors rarely achieve certainty about any proposition and must form an opinion and/or report in a position of relative uncertainty based on probability, according to the strength of the evidence. There is, of course, a minimum position of confidence which auditors must achieve to be able to form an opinion or to report. The significance of this postulate is that at some stage the cost of further evidence and of the resultant increased confidence which the auditors obtain must be measured against the enhanced social good which that would produce. This is explained and illustrated by Mautz and Sharaf (1961, p. 85):

> **cost and time are important; it would be unreasonable to incur substantial costs to ascertain the existence of assets of inconsequential amounts. It might also be unreasonable to incur substantial costs to prove the existence of assets of even significant amounts if other types of evidence are sufficiently persuasive and more readily available. The difference between compelling evidence and very persuasive evidence may not be sufficiently important to warrant the added cost of obtaining the former.**

It is important to remember, however, that there are a number of interests to take into account in most audits. Audit is part of the machinery of social control, and there is a societal interest to take into account in addition to the interests of the parties directly involved. It is, therefore, a total social benefit against social cost which has to be compared in considering the social justification for audit.

This postulate has important implications for the theory of audit evidence.

Summary

These basic postulates, which define and interpret the audit as a social phenomenon, provide the foundation for theoretical development. This divides into three main branches:

The source of audit authority and the concept of audit independence.
The audit process and the theory of audit evidence and criteria for reporting.
The standards of audit performance.

These are the areas in which a theoretical foundation and framework and the principles derived from these are necessary for the development of sound practice, and as a basis for testing the soundness and consistency of practice. An understanding of the theoretical content of these elements of auditing will also provide information about those fields of knowledge which must be studied to give auditors the competence to practise.

Authority

II

Introduction to Part II

Audit is a control function which monitors and reports on conduct, performance and achievement measured by reference to agreed criteria and compared with established norms of expectation, attesting the quality of information about an organisation required by persons who have no direct access to the source of the information and prepared by persons who have a vested interest in it. The auditors who carry out the audit express a personal opinion on the matters comprised within the terms of reference as a result of the examination which has been undertaken. The auditors' opinion must carry authority if it is to have a social utility: if it did not carry sufficient unquestioned authority it would add little to the unaudited information already available to the parties concerned. What, then, is the source of that authority which makes the opinion valuable?

The auditors' opinion is intended to assist the persons to whom it is addressed to form judgements and to take decisions by reason of the information it gives on the quality of the statements, accounts, conduct, performance or achievement of the persons or organisations involved. It does this by confirming the reliability and adequacy of information already presented by the persons or organisations, by providing additional information in appropriate cases, and by reporting those respects in which conduct, performance, or quality of information conforms with or deviates from a standard of expectation. It reflects favourably or unfavourably on how individuals have discharged their responsibilities.

These individuals hold their appointments because they have been judged fit to do so. The reasons for an audit of what they have done have been discussed in Part I and are further explained in Chapter 4. The audit is an essential element in the process of accountability, and the quality of it is important to both those who are the subject of the audit and those who are the recipients of the audit report. The rights and interests of the parties are potentially affected by the consequences resulting from the audit report: to fulfil the purpose of the audit, therefore, both these groups must believe in its authority. Any reservations about the technical quality, reliability, integrity or dependability of the audit would be prejudicial to the authority of the audit and therefore the acceptability of its outcome.

This means that there must be confidence in the technical competence, reliability and integrity of the auditors. Auditors who did not understand the subject matter of the audit or how to audit, and whose honesty, integrity and reliability were suspect, would be of little value to the parties. Where there is the potential for a conflict of interest between the parties in the subject matter of the audit or in the decisions taken on the basis of the audit, the utility of the audit is diminished if any party believes that the auditors may show a preference to any other. Auditors who were not believed to be sufficiently dependable to form an informed, honest and independent opinion would carry no authority with the parties. Authority is implicit in the theoretical concept of audit. Without authority there is little, if any, value in the audit. If the parties cannot accept the authority of the audit judgement – and acceptance of the authority does not mean that they necessarily agree with the judgement – there is no common premise for further action. Universal confidence and trust in the capacity of the audit are crucial. These are essential. Without this confidence and trust why should the auditors' opinion be thought to add anything of value to consideration of the accountability of the audited: without them how could the audited be expected to consider the auditors' opinion to be of any value? The social value of auditing stems from the fact that it does carry authority: without authority there would be constant conflict between the parties due to uncertainty or disagreement as to the true state of affairs.

The auditors' opinion is no more than an opinion, but it must be believed to be an informed opinion honestly held. It is to the source of that authority and confidence and belief in the capacity of the auditors to give an honest, informed opinion that we must now look.

In the simplest case it is no doubt a matter for the parties involved to satisfy themselves about the capacity of the auditors, but they are likely to use established common criteria. Where, however, the public interest is involved or the audit is a matter of public concern, the basis of authority and the capacity of the auditors are public, not private, issues. In both cases the principles are the same, but when the public interest is involved the arrangements require to be more formalised.

Consideration is therefore necessary of what the institutional arrangements are which can secure that the public can be assured that persons designated as auditors do have appropriate education, training and experience and a requisite level of competence; that auditors do have the requisite personal qualities of honesty, integrity and objectivity which support independence of judgement and opinion. There also needs to be consideration of what other conditions have to be established to sustain continuing confidence in the independence and integrity of the audit function.

Competence

3

The first requirement for the authority of auditors is competence. Audit competence requires both knowledge and skill, which are the products of education, training and experience.

The necessary education comprises general knowledge, knowledge of auditing principles, practices and procedures, and knowledge of the matters which are the subject of audit. Auditing is intellectually demanding, requiring a trained mind and the capacity for exercise of judgement. A broad general education cultivating the habit of systematic thinking and mental discipline, combined with a basic understanding of the principal fields of knowledge and ability for expression and communication orally and in writing, are an essential foundation.

Auditing itself has been defined as synoptic, drawing on other fields of knowledge but constituting a discipline on its own in the way that knowledge is adapted and applied to the issues of auditing. Auditing is an investigative process drawing on logic, mathematics and the behavioural sciences. In its methods of enquiry, use of evidence and deducing conclusions, it makes assumptions which are derived from these fields of knowledge and integrates them in a way which is peculiar to the phenomenon of auditing to enable it to fulfil its social function. However, auditing requires much more than a knowledge of its own theory or philosophy and the principles of its peculiar investigative process: it requires an understanding of the nature, structure, institutions and law of the society in which it is applied. And in

48

relation to particular audits it requires a knowledge of the activity in respect of which the conduct, performance or information has to be addressed.

Auditing and accounting tend to be associated. This is because almost universally in diverse organisations accountability is exacted for the custody and stewardship of financial resources, and in many organisations and especially in business firms accountability is demonstrated by the preparation of periodic accounts reporting on the custody, stewardship and management of these resources. Whatever else is expected of directors, managers, administrators, etc., they are expected to be accountable in financial terms, and auditors are expected to verify this. Auditors are required to be knowledgeable about accounting. Auditors in public practice, because of the skills required, are generally professional accountants, and the twin disciplines of accounting and auditing have developed in association. This, however, obscures the fact that there are two disciplines and that the scope of auditing goes much wider than financial accounts.

Audit of government, for example, includes not only the verification of financial records and accounts – the compliance audit – but is concerned also with economy and efficiency in the use of resources and with effectiveness in the achievement of policy objectives. For much, if not most, of this the performance indicators are not financial measures, and the requisite knowledge is not accounting. Typically, government auditors have not been predominantly accountants but have been specially trained as government auditors.

Management audit, operational audit and the audit of government, and of public institutions where the same criteria apply, require a multi-disciplinary approach, the emphasis of which is dependent on the particular activity that is being audited. There is scope for accountant-auditors to extend their range of knowledge to be able to demonstrate their competence in fields other than accounting, but because of the peculiar complexities in the technicalities of different services, and of specialisms in management and administration, the most responsible audits require some involvement of other specialists in more than one field. The development and understanding of performance indicators for areas such as education, health care, the police, refuse collection and the armed services, are each likely to require the range and depth of knowledge and experience possessed by a relevant specialist which is different from that of a specialist accountant.

The one common element in all accountability is financial accountability, and the breadth of knowledge of the diverse subject matter of audit which this gives, together with the highly developed investigatory and analytical skills and well-established independent professionalism of the accountant-auditor, makes a strong case for that person being the principal auditor, with such specialist assistance as each situation requires. It is not, however, a universal formula, and other specialists, if they have the knowledge and experience of auditing as a discipline and the independent professionalism which auditing as a practice requires, can act as auditors. But being a specialist does not make a person an auditor: education and training as an auditor and acceptance of the role of an auditor and the self-discipline which that imposes are also required. A knowledge of more than auditing and accounting is essential for the accountant-auditor, and the position is similar for any other specialists who, in addition to applying their special knowledge, skill and experience in execution of the audit tasks, undertake the role of auditor.

Because of the responsible and judgemental character of auditing, the significance of the consequences which flow from it, and the nature of the matters with which they must deal, auditors require a knowledge of accounting, statistics, computing and information systems, political economy, business economics, law, organisation theory, management, business policy and the functional specialisms of business (production, purchasing, labour and industrial relations, marketing and finance), administration, public policy, and the principles of government. Without this knowledge they do not have the competence to put the issues with which they will be confronted into proper context and perspective, and to judge their materiality in relation to the audit objective. It is obvious that not every issue will need the whole range of knowledge; and it is not suggested that the whole body of knowledge is divided into discrete elements. The auditors' knowledge in these fields should become integrated and synthesised so as to guide investigation, understanding and judgement.

The audit must carry authority: to carry authority all parties must have confidence in the audit: confidence requires that the parties believe that the audit has been carried out competently and that the auditors are capable of understanding the matters being dealt with. The audited, i.e. directors, managers, administrators, will not accept the judgement of auditors without reservation if they do not believe that they adequately understand the role and responsibilities of those who are audited, the unique features and complexities of their organisations, and the difficulties and problems with which they are faced. Similarly, if the audit report is to carry authority with those who receive it, they require to be confident that the auditors have the capability to make a thorough, informed and penetrating investigation and a competent judgement on the conduct and performance of the audited and/or a competent verification and appraisal of the information or accounts which they have prepared. Without that confidence of the parties the opinion of the auditors can add little in the process of securing accountability.

Since relevant competence is essential for confidence, the public need to have some means of distinguishing the competent from the incompetent. Audit competence requires auditors to have undergone a programme of dedicated education, training and experience. Auditors must, therefore, be able to demonstrate to the public that they have done so by obtaining a reputable qualification which vouches for the successful completion of such a programme. The standing of any qualification is the product of the reputation of the institution or organisation granting it and the result of public experience of the capability of those who hold it.

Audit is a matter of such social importance that the state has a responsibility to be satisfied in the public interest that appropriate standards of knowledge, training and experience are prescribed and that an adequate standard of proficiency is achieved. This is to ensure that, for the protection of the public whose property and other rights and interests are involved in relation to an activity for which advanced complex specialist skill and the exercise of judgement are involved, only those who are qualified in terms prescribed or recognised by the state are entitled to act.

This may be achieved by a state licensing system in which the state prescribes the curriculum of study, the educational standard, the requisite experience and a test of professional competence.

Alternatively, where there is a well organised and highly respected auditing profession, as in the United Kingdom where the tradition is for professions to be self-regulated, the state may grant recognised status to qualified members of professional bodies which have educational, experience and examination requirements which are satisfactory to the state.[1]

The state may then legislate that the audit of organisations specified may only be carried out by persons so licensed or recognised. The state's license or recognition is evidence of a satisfactory basic competence and capability. The relevant group which appoints an auditor is free to select from those licensed or recognised, an auditor or auditors whose personal reputation and experience commend themselves.

The difficulties of auditing in large organisations and the greater depth of specialised knowledge and skill which are required point to the need for some degree of audit specialisation. Some different divisions might be, for example, banks and other financial institutions, insurance, central government, regional and local government, sectors of manufacturing industry, and international groups. The principles of auditing are universally applicable, and qualified auditors recognised as such should be capable of applying and adapting their skills to a wide range of organisations. The call for specialisation depends on the basic thesis for audit authority. Auditors must have the relevant knowledge at a sufficient level to be able to audit the most senior officers of the organisation and to understand the greatest complexities of the organisation's activities. The range of organisations with which an individual auditor can deal is limited only by a personal capacity to master the specialties.

In organisations not so specified by the state, the parties concerned are free to appoint as auditors such persons as they please, but if they do not select persons who are recognised by the state as qualified they must decide independently the competence of their appointees.

Public recognition as qualified raises the question of what should be the terms of that recognition being continued from year to year. The continual evolution of auditing as a result of the expansion of knowledge in the relevant fields, changing concepts of accountability, increasing complexity and sophistication in organisations, management and administration, and enhanced public expectations, places an obligation on qualified auditors constantly to update their knowledge and skill. This is a question that is common to all learned professions. Can the continued competence of the practitioners be assumed until some failing is exposed, or should some system of monitoring or retesting be operated?

As will be discussed later, passive monitoring is essential for confidence in auditors to be maintained. Reported incompetence must be dealt with and be seen to be dealt with expeditiously and impartially in the public interest, with the ultimate sanction of withdrawal of recognition in appropriate cases. The status and authority of those who remain recognised is reaffirmed by the disciplining of those who have failed to maintain their standards.

Active monitoring by inspection and retesting of individuals may be felt to be ideal, but in the absence of a serious crisis of confidence such a procedure is unlikely to be cost effective. Satisfactory measures of quality control and performance review procedures which are dealt with in Chapter 11 are considered to be adequate measures in normal circumstances.

Programmes of continuing professional education assist practitioners in maintaining competence and skill. Whether these should be compulsory is arguable. The essential point is that practitioners must take some positive action, according to their own preference, which best suits their circumstances, to maintain the level of competence which recognition as qualified vouchsafes to the public.

Independence

4

Essential distinguishing characteristics of audit are the independence of its status and its freedom from investigatory and reporting constraints.

This is probably the most important of the audit postulates. The proposition of audit independence is universally supported. There is general recognition that the authority and the value of the investigation which is described as audit and of the report which results from that examination are products of and dependent on the degree of independence with which the investigation and report are made. Authority is, of course, also dependent on the knowledge, experience, skill and competence used, but the full benefit of these can only be derived if the audit is 'independent'. It is important, therefore, to understand what independence means and what it implies.

Audit independence is not a simple concept. Its attainment is the result of a combination of personal and organisational factors. Its nature and meaning are peculiar to the audit situation and derive from the purpose and objective of an audit. The special quality of independence which is sought as an essential distinguishing characteristic of audit is the product of the personal capacity of auditors to conduct themselves independently and of the absence of externally imposed constraints on the exercise of their independence. Audit independence is achieved only through the independence of auditors, and this can be circumscribed or compromised either through defects in their personal capacity or the imposition of restrictions on their freedom of investigation and reporting. The capacity of auditors to conduct themselves independently will be frustrated if the arrangements for audit limit their freedom to investigate and report; and unqualified freedom of investigation and reporting will not result in an independent audit if auditors are lacking in personal independence.

'Audit' implies 'independence', but since there are varying degrees of independence the term 'an independent audit' – although tautological – is used to signify an audit in which the two elements – personal independence and freedom of investigation and reporting – are both present, without reservation, restriction or limitation, and in which the 'external' organisational status of the auditor is emphasised. In an 'independent' audit the auditor is external to and not part of the organisation – i.e. independent of the audited organisation – as contrasted with the situation in an internal audit, which is conducted and controlled from within the organisation. The use of the term 'independent audit' underlines the constitutional separation from the organisational entity which is audited and the 'external' nature of the auditor's position. It is not, however, the constitutional separation itself which is important but the consequences which flow from it – or, the consequences which flow if the separation is absent.

The greater the responsibility or social significance of the audit, the more important it is that criteria of independence are satisfied. In those situations where the responsibility and social significance of the audit are at their greatest, as, for example, in state audit, audit of listed companies or audit of public boards or corporations, the criteria of independence must be applied with the greatest rigour. In other situations it is a matter of judgement as to how much, if any, relaxation or tolerance may be allowed from standards of independence without inhibiting achievement of the audit objective. These, however, are matters of practice, and it is to the concept of independence in a theoretical sense to which the following analysis and explanation are addressed.

It is the social function of the audit which creates the need for independence. The full potential of an audit cannot be realised if it is not wholly and truly independent; if it is not independent, the social purpose will be frustrated. The audit situation most commonly arises in those circumstances where there is a duty of accountability by persons who have, for example, responsibility for the custody, management, or power of disposal of financial and other economic resources, performance or provision of services. An audit is required because, as a consequence of the remoteness, complexity or significance of the operations, the persons to whom the accountability is due are dependent on reports for information about the utilisation of these resources, etc., and as the basis of acceptance or rejection, approval or disapproval of the conduct, etc., of the accountable persons, i.e. the audited.

The reports of these accountable persons have a value in the state in which they are prepared, and, whether or not in the form of reports, the information on conduct, performance, results or consequences which is given has a value on its own, since it demonstrates to some extent the way in which they have discharged their duty of custody, management or administration. There is an unavoidable potential conflict of interest where the accountable persons report on or control the disclosure of evidence on their performance or the utilisation and disposition of the resources entrusted to them. Assessment of conduct or performance may have unfavourable consequences for them. Accordingly, there is always the possibility of a tendency to avoid drawing attention to disappointing results, unavoidable or unforeseeable ill-fortune, and especially to incompetence, inefficiency or neglect. This may be bad enough, but where there is dishonesty, irregularity or uncorrected material error, there is a greater danger that efforts will be made to conceal it. The accountable persons, consciously or unconsciously, are likely to have a predisposition to present the facts in a way which is favourable to themselves or which supports their objectives, which may be different from or in conflict with those of the persons to whom they are accountable. It is because of this real or potential conflict that society seeks the assistance of audit in situations in which, because of the remoteness, complexity or significance of the subject matter, individuals have insufficient information, or insufficient access to verify the information, to enable them to judge for themselves.

The audit situation also arises where a person provides information for general or public interest, or as a basis of action or decision by some other persons, which reflects on the performance of the person preparing it, or in the quality of which the person preparing it has a vested interest, so that there is a potential conflict of interest such as to give grounds for doubt as to the reliability and credibility of that information. In such a situation, where the issue is significant and where the interested individuals whom it is sought to influence are unable to judge for themselves because of insufficient access to evidence or of remoteness or complexity of the subject matter, the preparer and the users of the information have a mutual interest to seek by the process of audit to improve the quality of the information and to create belief in its credibility and reliability.

The function of the audit in all cases is to investigate the facts and then, as appropriate, to attest to the quality of the report or the information, to attest to the honesty, regularity and standard of the conduct, performance or achievement, or provide additional information and opinion thereon to supplement what has already been disclosed. The objective is to provide an adequate basis for informed judgement by those to whom accountability is due or who have a need for and right to reliable information.

An auditor is a reporter, a specially qualified and skilled reporter, whose opinion has to be weighed with that of the audited. But an auditor is not the final judge of the issues. An auditor is a witness to the facts and in appropriate cases expresses an authoritative opinion on the facts. The responsibility rests with some other group as to what action follows – the shareholders of a company, the members of a club, the Public Accounts Committee in the case of central government departments, and so on. An auditor must be an objective and faithful reporter if the disability of remoteness or lack of access to information on the part of individuals who do have the authority and responsibility for action is to be overcome.

Auditors must, therefore, do more than put themselves in the place of the interested individuals to whom accountability is due, viewing events from their point of view and giving them the information which they would have sought for themselves. Auditors must be impartial. Auditors must be recognised as being without bias or partiality towards any interest. Auditors who were not independent of the audited would be of little value to the individuals to whom accountability was due, since there could be little confidence that their opinion added to what was already available. For example, the confirmation by a company director of a co-director's preparation of accounts and report thereon might be interesting and would establish that there was agreement among directors; however, such confirmation would add little if anything to the confidence of a shareholder who wanted reassurance that these accounts were properly prepared and free from directors' bias, fraud and irregularity; thus persons who are under the influence or instruction of, or in some way dependent on, the directors could not be thought to be properly qualified as that company's auditors. Similarly, auditors in whose impartiality the audited had no confidence would be unacceptable to them. They have to be prepared to submit their conduct and performance to examination with confidence in the fairness to them of the auditors' reporting. They may not always agree with the auditors, but they must have confidence that their opinion will be competently and honestly based solely on the evidence.

In cases where the report or information on conduct and performance has wider social significance than to the group to whom the report is immediately addressed or the information is released, the need for independence from all groups is most apparent. Objective standards of reporting and disclosure require dispassionate review of the reports and information which are represented as conforming to these standards.

Auditors, whatever personal and professional qualities are required of them, must also be independent in the sense of being absolutely without bias, personal interest in the outcome, prior commitment to an interest, or susceptibility to influence or pressure, any of which would lead any of the parties to believe that the report or opinion was determined other than by reference to the facts of the investigation alone. The report or opinion of an auditor is valueless if it does not carry authority with those who have to accept it, to use it and to rely on it. Auditors must therefore be demonstrably qualified for the task. It is vital that it should be patent that they have had the requisite education, training and experience to acquire the necessary skill, that they have demonstrated competence, and that they have acquired reputation and status. These qualities are essential as a basis for authority and acceptance. But the authority ultimately is critically dependent on the actual and perceived independence of the auditor or auditors in each individual situation.

If there is any reservation on the total independence of the auditors, if that independence is qualified, or compromised or circumscribed, there will be a consequential erosion of authority. The extent of the damage to authority will be related to the seriousness of the reservation or compromise in the perception of any of the parties in relation to the objectives of the audit and the use which is to be made of the audit report or opinion.

Internal auditors in a company, for example, are not totally independent since they are employees of the company and ultimately subject to instruction from the directors and management. But within a prescribed sphere they can be given unqualified independence, reporting to directors on areas of responsibility of those subordinate to the directors. Internal auditors' independence, while not total in an absolute sense, can be total in relation to the circumstances of the particular appointment so that their report is not only unbiased, but accepted as such by all parties involved. It must be so if they are to fulfil their role.

Independence, therefore, is not a concept which lends itself to universal constitutional prescription, but one for which the constitutional prescription will depend on what is necessary to satisfy the criteria of independence in the particular circumstances.

The independence of auditors is the product of the combination of personal qualities, organisational arrangements and environmental circumstances or constraints. It is how auditors act and the conditions under which they act which determine whether it is possible for them to be independent, whether they are in fact independent, and whether they are perceived to be independent. It is on these factors that belief in the independence of the audit will depend.

4.1 Mental Attitude

It is frequently asserted that independence is a question of mental attitude or state of mind. This is important. It is a state of independence of thought and action which must be achieved and which must be brought to bear in the execution of the audit. This is the objective – to attain and preserve the mental attitude which results in independence on the part of auditors and belief in that independence by those who rely on them. It is not sufficient only for auditors to be independent, for them to think and to act independently. They are reporting to others whose benefit is derived from the reassurance which they give and whose reassurance is conditional on belief in the auditors' independence. The reality of the auditors' independence must be apparent to them. The circumstances must, therefore, be such as to make it possible for auditors to sustain their independence, for them successfully to resist and reject anything which would impair or be prejudicial to that independence, and these circumstances must be open and unconcealed, and be seen to be such as should sustain independence. There can be no guarantee that independence will be achieved and sustained, because the actuality is dependent on an auditor's judgement and decision in the circumstances. But the circumstances must be such that an auditor who wishes to be independent is protected from prejudicial conditions, influences or pressures, and that this protection is apparent.

The mental attitude which is a condition of or conducive to independence in auditing requires something more than the right environmental circumstances, however. The capacity for such a mental attitude is an attribute of character which has ethical or moral connotations. The mental attitude required by auditing demands probity of character and belief in and adherence to an ethical code of behaviour, and a public reputation for those attributes of character. These personal qualities, which are difficult to define and inculcate, rank ahead of the organisational constraints which are prescribed if auditor independence is to be achieved. The position which must be achieved by the organisational constraints is that an auditor with the right personal and professional qualities must be absolutely without bias, personal interest in the outcome, prior commitment to an interest, susceptibility to influence or pressure, or restriction on freedom to investigate and report, any of which would lead any of the parties to believe that the reported opinion was determined other than by reference to the facts of the investigation alone.

It is necessary to consider, therefore, the circumstances which could exert improper influence or pressure on an auditor, which could give rise to a personal interest in the outcome of an audit, which could occasion prior commitment to an interest, which could impose restrictions on investigating and reporting, or which could induce bias in an auditor's investigation, opinion or report.

The position which has been defined and which it is proposed to examine in some detail is, of course, an ideal or perfect state of affairs. It remains to be seen whether or to what extent the ideal is capable of achievement, or whether the cost of its total achievement is disproportionate to the benefit, i.e. whether the marginal benefit of greater assurance or confidence that would be lost by some sacrifice of the ultimate rigour is more than compensated by some other consequential benefit or cost saving. Is it indeed possible for an individual to have a completely 'sterile' mind, without any bias, produced by the circumstances of their upbringing, education, cultural tradition, political belief, and so on? However, these are issues which will be returned to later. It is necessary first to look at the conditions and constraints which create, support and foster audit independence.

4.2 Public Belief in Independence

It is important to appreciate that effective audit independence cannot be created by edict. Effective audit independence requires confidence in that independence by the users, the recipients of the audit opinion or report. The natural approach of the users is one of scepticism. Why should users believe that auditors have not succumbed to all the improper influences to improve their own position, which adherence to the constraints of independence would deny them? User scepticism can be overcome and confidence engendered by the reputation of auditors for independent thought and action, and by observance that auditor behaviour is monitored and that sanctions are imposed for departure from established norms. The supervision of auditor behaviour and the administration of sanctions may be imposed by a self-regulatory system as in the United Kingdom, or by a state agency; the important point is that for user confidence it must be seen to be effective.

A reputation, however, can only be established over time by conduct and performance. Similarly, the credibility of a system of monitoring is the product of a record of achievement in the fulfilment of declared objectives. There is no such thing as 'instant' audit independence. But once social acceptance is obtained, the concept of audit independence becomes institutionalised and an 'auditor' enjoys the benefit of a vicarious reputation, provided use of the designation is sufficiently restricted. The complementary proposition, however, is also true that every auditor, by his or her actions, conduct and performance, can enhance or damage the institutionalised concept, with potential consequences for every other auditor. All persons who hold themselves out to be auditors have, therefore, a common interest in protecting the institutional reputation as well as their own, if the social utility of a service which they offer is to be maintained. Society for its part also has an interest in ensuring that auditors' reputation for independence is protected, otherwise the social benefit of the service will be lost. Society and auditors have, therefore, a common interest in excluding from employment as auditors, persons who do not accept the discipline of the constraints imposed by the concept of independence. There is also a common interest in not describing as an audit an examining or investigating process in which the investigator is insufficiently independent, either personally or organisationally.

It is, perhaps, paradoxical that the factors which influence the capacity of auditors for independence have been described as constraints. They do impose restrictions on the circumstances in which an audit can be carried out, and on persons who aspire to audit, even if they have the personal qualities, education, training and experience to enable them to do the necessary work. But the purpose of the restrictions is to ensure that in relation to an audit, the auditor is unrestricted.

The fundamental principles are twofold. First, any circumstance which has influenced, or which has the appearance of having been likely to have influenced, the mental attitude of an auditor adversely in striving for objectivity and impartiality, or which has the potential for doing so, or appearing to do so, is offensive to the concept of independence, and is objectionable. Second, any circumstance which puts impediment in the way of an auditor's investigation of the facts and reporting on them, or which appears to do so, or which has or appears to have the potential to do so, is offensive to the concept of independence, and is objectionable.

4.3 Circumstances Material to Independence

Illustrative circumstances which are material in relation to audit independence or its perception can be conveniently classified and examined under five headings:

1. Personal qualities.
2. Personal relationships.
3. Financial interest or dependence.
4. Investigative and reporting freedoms.
5. Organisational status.

The nature of the relevant circumstances under each of these headings can be defined, and the importance of them examined in detail. Any departure from the ideal, or shortcoming in meeting it, must result in prejudice to or compromise of independence. How damaging the prejudice or compromise will be will depend on the circumstances. The importance of any reduction in independence needs to be considered in relation to the audit objective. Although audit independence is of primary importance for audit authority and social value, as has already been indicated, some sacrifice of these may be justified by a net social gain from the circumstances which compromised the independence. Other social benefits may be sufficient to enable acceptance of some loss of authority due to the absence of complete independence, provided the maximum independence possible in the circumstances is achieved and the nature and extent of the shortcoming in independence is disclosed to or known by the parties involved. Reference will be made again to this question. It is sufficient to note at this stage that while independence is central to the concept of audit and the basis of confidence in and authority of audit opinion, independence is the means to an end and not the end itself. If confidence sufficient for the audit objective can be established by other means, some sacrifice may be accepted to enable other social benefits to be obtained. Nevertheless, as a general principle, absolute independence should be the objective. Where it cannot be achieved the parties must be aware of the circumstances.

Personal qualities

The two most essential personal qualities for an auditor are probity and strength of character. However technically skilled and competent in auditing individuals may be, if they have uncertain moral or ethical standards there must be doubt as to whether they can sustain the mental attitude essential to the audit approach, particularly in situations where the pressures and influences on impartiality are greatest. Similarly, persons of weak and vacillating character cannot be relied on to sustain the mental attitude of impartiality and hold to their views against pressure from a person of determined, dominating or overbearing personality whose conduct or performance is subject of audit. These qualities may be difficult to define or prescribe, but they are listed first because they are of first importance. The organisational and procedural conditions considered below will be of little avail if the personal integrity of the auditor cannot be relied on.

The personal reputation of auditors for probity is supported by the institutional status of auditing as a profession. Persons recognised as members of the auditing profession are believed to have accepted the obligations of professionalism in regard to their conduct and concern for the public interest; they are expected to conform to a code of ethics and to be subject to sanctions in the event of their failing to do so. Public confidence in the capacity of an auditor for independence is dependent in part on the personal repute of the individual and in part on belief in their professionalism. The matter of professionalism and ethics is dealt with more fully in Chapter 5.

Personal relationships

The principle here is clear enough; it stems from a recognition of the difficulties of conflict of interest, or conflict of loyalties, or emotional involvement in a situation which calls for objectivity, impartiality and detachment. A person is disqualified from acting as auditor if a personal relationship exists which would be liable to influence their mental attitude, judgement or opinion, or which might appear to do so. For example, a person may not act as auditor in a situation in which a spouse, parent or child has an interest in the outcome. The situation created by an immediate relative is obvious, but it is more difficult to decide as a generality how far in kinship there is a potential conflict and, therefore, how far the prohibition should go. Similarly, a person may not act as auditor in a situation in which they or their employer, or their employee or partner or co-director has an interest in the outcome. These are legal relationships which can be identified and defined. Other examples may be quoted. The bond of loyalty or emotion with a personal friend can be as strong, or stronger, than any of these. It is the principle which is important and which must be recognised. The disqualifying relationships do not stop at those which can be defined and proscribed by rules. The potentiality of conflict must be recognised and acted on.

A person is disqualified to act as auditor if they have any reason to believe that the circumstances are such that a personal relationship has or will appear to have the potential to exert an improper pressure, damaging to their mental attitude, or exercise of judgement and expression of opinion.

Receipt of personal favours, gifts or privileges by an auditor at the instance of those whose intromissions or performance are under examination is damaging to audit independence. It does not matter whether the intention in extending such favours, etc. is to influence the mental attitude of the auditor. The reality is that, consciously or unconsciously, the auditor's attitude may be influenced favourably towards the persons under examination. Equally objectionable, the fact that favours, gifts or privileges have been accepted may lead others to believe that the mental attitude of the auditor has been influenced. This is a particularly difficult area. While working contact between auditor and audited requires a certain rapport and inevitably produces the ordinary cordiality of social intercourse, the auditor must endeavour to maintain a professional detachment. Tangible expressions of appreciation of a good professional relationship or the extension of ordinary employee benefits (e.g. sales discounts or other facilities) to audit staff may be unlikely to have a sinister purpose. They have, however, the potential, insidiously and unconsciously, to corrupt the detachment of the audit approach and to influence judgement at the margin. They are likely to be seen in this light by those who have to rely on the audit.

Financial interest or dependence

An auditor's financial interest in the subject matter of audit or in the outcome of the audit would undoubtedly be a potential source of conflict of interest and of improper pressure on his or her mental attitude, exercise of judgement and unbiased opinion. In principle, not only the actuality but also the potentiality of such a conflict of interest is objectionable to the concept of audit independence. Any financial interest is, accordingly, in absolute terms a disabling characteristic for an auditor. In practical terms, without the sacrifice of principle, the degree of disablement is dependent on the materiality of the interest. Mental attitude is most unlikely to be affected where the financial interest is obviously trivial and no threat to actual independence arises. The materiality of the interest has to be measured, however, by reference not only to the influence on the auditor but also to the effect on the user. A financial interest which may not appear material to an auditor may be damaging to the appearance of independence and may be instrumental in destroying the user's belief in that independence. The auditor's opinion may be sound because there is no reason for their mental attitude to be affected, but the opinion might be suspect because of lack of user confidence. So the purpose of the audit and the social benefit are frustrated. A person must not act as auditor in a situation in which he or she identifies a conflict or potential conflict because of financial interest, but this is not the only consideration. It is the user's perception of the situation that is critical.

The issue of principle is that a circumstance which has the capacity to affect the personal financial position of an auditor – adversely or favourably – is a threat to audit independence and accordingly a disabling factor as auditor for the person affected.[1]

Circumstances in which this issue commonly arises include:

(a) Investment by auditor.
(b) Borrowing by auditor.
(c) Settlement of auditor remuneration.
(d) Auditor beneficiary.
(e) Disproportionate fee dependence on audited organisation.

These are illustrative only: it is the question of principle of financial interest or dependence producing conflict of interest that is important.

(a) Investment by auditor

The threat to independence or actual damage arises from the effect on the mental attitude of an auditor of their having an investor's interest in the organisation which is subject to audit. As an investor an auditor has an interest in the consequence for capital and for income of the performance of the organisation in which the investment has been made. The issue is whether such an investor interest is potentially the source of conflict of interest operating consciously or unconsciously on the mind of the auditor, affecting their attitude to matters of difficulty which arise in the audit. An auditor's function is to investigate and to report objectively and impartially. The issue is whether a disposition to protect or improve their own personal position as investor would affect that objectivity and impartiality, leading to a bias in deciding between alternative views on disputable items. The danger is that an auditor might, even unconsciously have a predisposition more readily to accept the explanation which was more favourable to him- or herself. Equally important, it is likely to appear to an interested third party that this is likely to be so, resulting in damage to the appearance of independence and the loss of user confidence. Decisions of directors or management on changes of policies as to depreciation, stock valuation, profit recognition, etc. which have an effect on dividend or dividend cover, earnings per share, interest cover, gearing ratio, and so on which are based on properly justifiable grounds, may be made in circumstances which require consideration of what really was the primary objective.

In principle the issue is clear. Investment in the audited organisation is objectionable to audit independence and is a disabling characteristic for an auditor. However, the objective is independence of thought and action, and an investment is objectionable only when it has the potential to produce a conflict of interest which may affect mental attitude. There can be no universal quantitative criteria for measuring this because of the variety of circumstances. While total absence of investment removes all doubt, it has to be recognised that it is the potential to produce a conflict of interest which is the criterion. Accordingly, for example, an investment which is trivial in relation to an auditor's resources is unlikely to be or seen to be damaging.

(b) Borrowing by auditor

The threat to independence or actual damage stems from the pressure which may be brought to bear on an auditor, affecting their freedom of investigation and or report, by reason of the relationship of debtor and creditor between the auditor and the audited organisation. Any relationship which has the potential of exposing an auditor to pressure which may prejudice the outcome of the audit is objectionable. The sense of personal obligation which an auditor might feel towards an accommodating lender, or the risk of personal embarrassment and difficulty which a lender could cause to a borrowing auditor by discriminatory action – for example, by recalling advances or raising interest rates – have the potential to produce a conflict of interest which could be used by unscrupulous persons who had acted or proposed to act in a way which the auditor should object to or disclose. The existence of the relationship, even if no pressure has been applied or is likely to be applied, is damaging to user confidence, since the appearance of independence is compromised. In this case also materiality is a factor, and borrowing which is trivial in relation to an auditor's resources is unlikely to be or seen to be damaging. In view of the subjectivity of defining materiality limits the situation is best totally avoided.

(c) Auditor remuneration

Auditors require to be paid for auditing. If any of the parties who have an interest in the audit are in a position to influence the size of the payment it can be argued that they are in a position to bring pressure to bear on the auditor, which will affect their mental attitude, thus prejudicing their independence. At the least, the appearance of absolute independence will be compromised. One of the fundamental principles of audit independence stated above is that any circumstance which puts impediment in the way of an auditor's investigation of the facts and reporting on them is objectionable. The important point here is that imposition of a financial limit is an interference with an auditor's freedom of investigating and reporting. This creates a difficult dilemma.

The technical nature of auditing and the personal professional judgement required in deciding the extent and nature of investigation that is necessary to support an opinion are such that the quality of the work is not susceptible to evaluation by a 'lay' person. Auditors must have freedom of investigation and reporting without financial constraint. Auditors must carry out a sufficiently extensive investigation to meet the societal objective of the audit, to discharge their professional obligation, and to support their opinion or report without going beyond what is necessary to meet the legal requirements of due care, the professional standard of diligence, and the economic cost–benefit test. These are all tests on which it is the auditor who must exercise judgement. A constraint on the responsible exercise of that judgement is an interference with the investigative freedom and therefore with the independence of the auditor. Yet whoever settles the payment must be satisfied that it is appropriate for the services rendered. Otherwise the system is open to the danger that the audit service expands beyond the needs of society, of which auditors should not be the sole judges, or to the allegation that 'auditors themselves fix the amount of their own remuneration'.

Government must exercise control over public expenditure; it must also provide funds to finance state audit, and since it could thereby restrict the extent of audit, the independence of the state auditor is at risk unless satisfactory arrangements are made to protect it. Public boards and company boards are the subject of audit and must also exercise control over expenditure: if they must authorise payment of the auditor's remuneration and are therefore in a position to control it, the independence of the auditor is at risk.

Different countries have made different arrangements to protect the investigative and the reporting freedom of state audit, but, even if the personal independence of the principal audit officer is assured, the extent of the auditing they can engage in is circumscribed by the numbers and/or quality of their staff, for which the state must grant the funds. A government is able, therefore, to influence the scope and intensity of audit by withholding funds or by reducing or declining to increase them.

The protection of the public is assured only by the freedom of the principal auditor to speak out frankly and fearlessly, informing and alerting the public to the government's interference with effective arrangements to ensure its own financial and other accountability.

Company and public boards have the means potentially to exert objectionable pressure on auditors if they have the responsibility of authorising payment of the auditors' remuneration. The pressure may be overt or covert, and the influence experienced by auditors may be conscious or unconscious. A generally hostile atmosphere and acrimony over fee settlements – where extension of the audit work may be most necessary – has the potential to condition auditors to do marginally less work, in the knowledge that further work will not be remunerated. This does not necessarily result in a conscious decision to curtail the audit programme but may unconsciously produce a reluctance to go beyond the minimum interpretation of the requirements of due diligence. In some respects, this is the more dangerous situation, where there is no intention on the part of auditors to do other than fulfil their audit obligation, or to allow financial constraint, and the penalty it imposes, to interfere with the conscientious discharge of audit duty with due diligence. There is a difficult balance to be held between properly constraining the audit within economic limits and frustrating the social purpose by an over-rigorous curtailment of imaginative and progressive initiatives. The danger is that due diligence is construed minimally. The easier situation to identify and to deal with is the overt and explicit hostility to the audit and payment for it. In such cases an auditor's remedy is to report to those persons whose interest lies in an effective audit.

In limited companies in the United Kingdom the matter is dealt with constitutionally by giving shareholders the power and responsibility to fix the audit remuneration. Since in practice this is generally delegated by the shareholders to the directors, there must be some doubt about the effectiveness of this protection to auditor independence. The fact that shareholders have the ultimate sanction may be more cosmetic than real. With the institution of audit committees – a committee of the board of directors composed mainly of non-executive directors – some additional protection has been claimed by giving such committees the task of agreeing the audit remuneration. It is suggested that this curtails the power of executive management to interfere with audit investigative and reporting freedoms through control of remuneration. The effectiveness of this is debatable because of the interdependence, joint responsibility and solidarity of board members. It may result in some improvement, but if there is a real issue of importance it does not get to the root of the matter. Non-executive directors are also subject to audit, and they too could have their own reasons for wishing to exert influence on an auditor.

One solution that has been suggested is that for public companies the audit should be conducted by a state audit service paid for by central government, so that the absolute financial independence of auditors would be assured. Quite apart from other considerations relative to the desirability of state audit for public limited companies, this solution does not solve the problem: it changes it. Auditors may then become subject to state or political pressure or direction, which may be even more objectionable.

This question is related to the arrangements for the appointment of auditors and it will therefore be examined further below. Since patronage is a potential source of pressure and therefore a threat to audit independence, the objective of the arrangements for appointment and remuneration must be to neutralise the pressures so far as they cannot be eliminated, and to have representatives of all interested parties involved, so that their confidence in the independence of the auditors will be assured. The real issue is sustaining confidence in the ability of auditors to remain independent.

(d) Auditor beneficiary

The existence of a relationship in which a person is in a position to benefit financially or from the use of facilities or otherwise as a result of a discretion exercised in their favour by the directors, managers or administrators of an organisation, is objectionable to the concept of audit independence of that person. Such a relationship produces a conflict of interest which has the potential to affect the mental attitude of an auditor consciously or unconsciously, interfering with their capacity for impartiality and objectivity and to expose them to pressure damaging to their investigative or reporting freedoms. Furthermore, it is damaging to the appearance of independence and detrimental to user confidence.

(e) Disproportionate fee dependence

A further potential source of undue pressure, conscious or unconscious, on auditors in public practice is dependence on one audited organisation for a major part of income. If that part of an auditor's income is sufficiently important that withdrawal of it would have serious personal consequences for the auditor, then the auditor is vulnerable to the threat of its cessation, with consequential effect on mental attitude and investigative and reporting freedoms. The understandable desire of auditors to please and not to alienate those persons who are responsible for their appointment has the potential to incline them, consciously or unconsciously, to favour too readily solutions to difficult audit problems which accord with the interests of those persons, without that degree of detachment, objectivity and impartiality which discharge of the audit function demands. This situation has the particular danger that it is likely to be concealed and not be apparent to the user groups who depend on the audit.

These illustrations of financial interest or dependence are indicative of the circumstances which have the potential to affect the mental attitude of auditors and/or to be prejudicial to their unrestricted freedom of investigating and reporting. There are, no doubt, other circumstances which have financial consequences for auditors and which might impair or be seen to impair their independence of thought and action. Any circumstances of this kind must be objectionable to audit independence and a disabling characteristic as auditor for a person affected by them.

Investigative and reporting freedoms

It has already been said that an auditor must be an objective and faithful reporter if the disability of remoteness or lack of access to information on the part of those individuals who rely on the audit report is to be overcome. Auditors must be impartial and recognised to be impartial. Their function is to investigate the facts and then to attest to the quality of a report or information which has been prepared by others, and/or to the honesty and regularity of conduct, or to provide additional information and opinion on the conduct, performance or achievement of persons who are subject to audit. The objective is to provide an adequate basis for informed judgement. The only basis on which auditors can make an unqualified attestation, report or opinion which will satisfy the needs and expectations of users and fulfil the social function of the audit, is that they should have an unrestricted right of access to all relevant information which exists and which they believe is necessary, and that they should be subject to no constraints in attesting, reporting or expressing their opinion as they think appropriate as a result of their investigation. Any impairment of these freedoms of investigation and reporting reduces the value of the audit and, if the impairment is sufficiently great, ultimately frustrates the purpose completely by destroying user confidence. Interference by any other person in the investigation or report introduces a bias which is in conflict with the principles of objectivity and impartiality. By their interference that person shows an interest in influencing the outcome which is in conflict with the expectation of independence of thought and action which other interested parties have of auditors. Freedom of investigation and reporting means that, once the audit objective has been defined in the audit terms of reference, auditors cannot accept from any person, and particularly from any person who is subject to the audit,

1. instructions
    (a) as to what shall or shall not be subject to audit investigation;
    (b) as to how the audit investigation shall be carried out; or
    (c) as to what evidence shall be obtained or accepted;
2. supervision or review of the audit proposed or performed with a view to passing judgement on its appropriateness;
3. instructions as to what the audit report will contain (or will not contain!) and/or how it will be expressed.

Auditors have an individual professional responsibility to carry out such investigation and to obtain and examine such evidence as they alone think necessary to enable them to discharge the terms of reference of the audit appointment; also to report completely and explicitly, as required by the terms of reference and as evidenced by the audit investigation. The terms of reference are not always the same, and it is the individual responsibility of an auditor to determine what is required by way of investigation, evidence and report in each case. There are recognised standards of professional competence and performance to which auditors must conform, and this subject is dealt with in some detail later. However, within that framework auditors must have the freedom to do what they believe is necessary.

Denial of access to records, documents or oral explanations must raise doubts in the mind of an auditor about the effect of knowledge which is being withheld. The objective of instruction, supervision or review by another party, particularly one who is subject to audit, must be to influence an auditor in forming an opinion about the need for access to or the relevance of records, documents and oral explanations which have been or might be examined which is an indirect interference with access. This must also raise doubts in the mind of an auditor as to the motives behind such an intention. These doubts can only be resolved by obtaining access or by removing the restrictions or pressures on access. Otherwise, the audit independence is impaired.

The auditor's report is intended to communicate so that those persons who are entitled to take action or who are responsible for taking action may do so on the basis of the information which is sought from the auditor and which the audit was instructed to obtain. Interference with the report must have as its objective altering the communication and so influencing that action to a course different from what would have resulted without that interference. This is a distortion of the audit report and a frustration of the audit purpose. It is in conflict with the independence of thought and action expected of an auditor and accordingly an objectionable interference.

Freedom of reporting includes unrestricted publication of the audit report to all those persons who have a legitimate right to receive it. In the case of the audit of departments of central government, local government authorities or public boards the public interest requires that the audit reports are public documents. In the case of other organisations the extent of public accountability will dictate what publication is necessary in the public interest. For example, in the case of limited companies, annual accounts must be filed with the Registrar of Companies, with the auditors' report attached, and accounts may not be circulated without the auditors' report. In other cases the extent of public circulation necessary in order to discharge the social purpose of the audit is a matter for consideration.

Organisational status

The constitutional and organisational arrangements for the appointment of auditors and for carrying out an audit are vitally important to the independence of auditors. These arrangements may be either supportive of or prejudicial to independence. The arrangements themselves will not make an auditor independent. That is a personal matter for auditors; it is a matter of their mental attitude and of their exercising independence of thought and action. An auditor may be independent in spite of the arrangements, but unsatisfactory arrangements will make it more difficult or even impossible to have all the freedom which is associated with independence; and unsatisfactory arrangements may be, and almost certainly will be, prejudicial to the appearance of independence. The user's perception of the independence of the auditor and of the audit carried out, conditions user confidence in the reliability, credibility and authority of the audit report.

The audit report is of limited value to the user if there is only qualified belief in the personal independence of the auditor and in their freedom to investigate and to report without instruction or restriction. It is important, therefore, to establish the constitutional and organisational conditions which are to be satisfied to secure audit independence. The objective again is to secure that auditors are not exposed to pressure, either overt or indirect, which could affect their mental attitude, consciously or unconsciously, so as to be prejudicial to the impartiality and objectivity of their investigation or report, or which could induce others to believe that this might be so; and that no impediment can be placed in the way of an auditor's freedom to investigate and report. Reference has already been made to the arrangements necessary to secure the conditions which safeguard or promote those aspects of independence which have been dealt with. There are other matters to be considered which fall into two groups:

(a) conditions of appointment
(b) conditions of operation

(a) Conditions of appointment

In any audit situation there are two or more groups who have an interest in the outcome of the audit. The persons who are subject to audit have an interest to secure that their conduct and performance are judged to be satisfactory according to whatever criteria are used, or that information prepared by them is attested as conforming satisfactorily to relevant criteria. The persons to whom the audit report is addressed may fall into one group, but they are more likely to divide into several groups, with different interests and priorities. Not all the groups will necessarily be specified as addressees, but for this purpose they include all those with a legitimate legal, social or moral right to be interested in the quality of conduct, performance or achievement of those entrusted with the direction, management or administration of the organisation which is subject to audit, or in the quality of the information which is subject to audit.

Some person or persons must appoint the auditor. The basic principle is that the appointment should not be made by persons whose position may be affected by the outcome of the audit and/or who have an interest in influencing the auditors in their investigation or report. If auditors are in a position where they are dependent for their appointment on such persons, they are potentially exposed to pressure or influence. The possibility of their being affected by pressure or influence is certainly damaging to the appearance of independence. Such a possibility also may, consciously or unconsciously, affect their mental attitude, with a real loss of independence because of lack of objectivity and impartiality. The actual exercise of pressure or influence is of course wholly objectionable.

The purpose of an audit is to benefit the group whose interests are served by instructing the audit. The terms of reference are devised to provide that benefit and serve that interest. The terms of reference are the instructions of the relevant interest group or groups. An auditor must receive that initial instruction from some quarter; 'audit' does not have a universal meaning. It requires to be related to the particular situation and the requirements of the relevant interest group or groups. Receipt of that initial instruction is not prejudicial to audit independence, provided it does not try to circumscribe investigative and reporting freedom in the discharge of what is stated to be the audit objective. Arrangements for the appointment of an auditor, and for defining the audit objective and terms of reference by the persons who seek to benefit from the audit, are not prejudicial to audit independence solely by reason of those persons having that power. The arrangements must, however, include provision for the protection of the auditor from improper pressure or influence on the part of the group or any one of the groups with whom the power of appointment lies. All the groups who receive the audit report have an interest in the audit, and it is conceivable that any one or more of them, if in a position to do so, could endeavour to bring pressure or influence to bear on the auditor to bias the investigation or report to favour the interests of the pressurising group, that the mental attitude of the auditor could be affected, consciously or unconsciously, by the potentiality of the situation, or that the perception of independence by other interested persons could be affected by the potentiality of the situation.

Placing the responsibility for the appointment of an auditor with the persons who are subject to audit is prejudicial to audit independence. Directors or the management of a company, for example, should not appoint the auditor who is to report to shareholders or other external groups on their reports or their conduct or performance. The prevalent practice in the United Kingdom of shareholders delegating to directors the responsibility of appointing the auditor is in principle objectionable. The fact that shareholders retain the power not to endorse the directors' recommendation and have on occasion exercised it does not ensure that the practice invariably operates in the public interest in all other cases. The institutionalising of the practice in recent years by the procedure of directors entertaining competitive presentations from a number of auditors as a basis for making a selection has the potential for even greater threats to auditor independence. While neither competition nor the practice of such presentations which include an outline of the audit and a fee quotation are themselves objectionable, the procedure gives the directors the opportunity to exercise improper influence on the freedom of investigation and pressure on the fee. Directors who have an interest in minimising the scope and depth of the audit and the amount of the audit fee, and who make a selection wholly or primarily on that basis, are not necessarily serving the interests of the parties who depend on the auditor. Particularly if they act from improper motives, they are able to influence the audit and at the same time present themselves as having a proper regard for cost effectiveness. An auditor who accepts an appointment at less than an economic fee for the work and responsibility involved, in the expectation of recovering any 'discount' by later increased fees on a continuing appointment, has immediately compromised independence. A vested interest in re-appointment has the potential to produce a conscious or unconscious predisposition to avoid confrontation with the directors on matters of difficulty or difference of opinion.

For shareholders alone to have the responsibility is hardly practicable, and in any event raises other reservations. Company auditors who are appointed primarily to report to shareholders under arrangements which are entirely satisfactory for their independence, are likely to be perceived by other interest groups as the shareholders' auditors and to be suspected of having a shareholder bias unless these groups are parties to the arrangements for the appointment. Employees and their representatives whose short-term and/or long-term interests are likely to be seen to be in conflict with those of the shareholders are unlikely to accept the shareholders' auditors also reporting to them unless they are satisfied that the arrangements for appointment ensure complete impartiality and objectivity and absolute independence from all groups. The directors and management, in their own interests and as representatives of the company with a regard for the company's interest, have a concern to be confident of the competence of the auditors and the disinterestedness of their approach.

As already stated above in relation to remuneration, the arrangements should be such as to neutralise the pressures so far as they cannot be eliminated, and have all parties involved so that their respective confidence in the independence of the auditors will be assured. The parties who have an interest include not only the shareholders, directors, managers and the company. The employee interest and the public interest need to be recognised.

In similar fashion, the appointment of a state auditor should not be in the hands of government, and local government auditors should not be appointed by permanent officials or elected representatives: auditors of public boards or government agencies should not be appointed by the board or the agency or by the responsible minister who has a political interest in the result. In each case the relevant interest groups must be identified so that an appropriate arrangement can be devised. This may involve putting the appointment in the hands of an independent agency.

The role of auditors has to be appreciated by all parties to be one of disinterested detachment, concerned with the issues but aloof from resolution of the conflict. An auditor is not an advocate for any of the parties. If the parties require a partisan commitment to their interest in a conflict it is not to the auditor that they should turn.

The overriding principle in all cases is that the audit is a totally independent function, and all parties with an interest require to be convinced of and have confidence in the integrity, impartiality and objectivity of auditors or the social purpose will be frustrated.

Once appointed, the principal measures for the protection of the auditors include irremovability during the tenure of the appointment – except for misconduct – and the right of auditors to make a public statement to all relevant interest groups, in the event of circumstances which appear to them to be prejudicial to the fulfilment of the audit objective.

(b) Conditions of operation

The matters for consideration here are the circumstances affecting the actual work of the audit which are prejudicial to the required mental attitude, the independence of thought and action, the impartiality and objectivity, and the freedoms of investigating and reporting which are essential to an audit; and the circumstances which are prejudicial to their appearance to and confident belief in them by the parties concerned.

One of the most important circumstances potentially affecting the independence of auditors or the perception of it is the involvement of auditors in other work, especially work which does not require the special independent characteristics of audit. The question is whether persons who engage in auditing are able to act with the independence which auditing requires and be perceived to do so, if they also engage in other work for which disinterested detachment is not required or which involves commitment to an interest. Are they able to act with the independence which auditing requires if they have been previously involved in a non-audit capacity with the matters or the persons that are the subject of audit, and will it appear to the relevant parties that auditors can do so? Do auditors damage their capacity and reputation for independence by also having a capacity and reputation for commitment to any of the interests which may be in conflict in an audit and between which auditors must be and be seen to be neutral? Is there any class of work of which auditors are capable which is incompatible with their status as auditors? The question is one of unqualified confidence in the authority of auditors and in the independence of auditors, i.e. capacity for independent thought and action. Two sets of circumstances are distinguishable. Firstly, when the other work is done for the same organisation as the audit. Secondly, when the other work is done for organisations other than those which are audited.

While the issue is one of principle which has a relevance in all audit situations, it arises most acutely for auditors in public practice. Auditors in public practice, at least in English-speaking developed countries, are generally in public practice as professional accountants, with auditing only one branch of a varied professional practice. Auditors in the public service – with central or local government – may, but are less likely to, be engaged in the provision of services other than audit; if they are, the same question of potential conflict arises. It also arises in the case of persons employed in an audit capacity within organisations: their capacity for independence, in the context of their audits, is potentially prejudiced by engagement in non-audit services.

The basic question which arises is whether involvement in another capacity consciously or unconsciously influences the mental attitude of an auditor, introduces a personal interest in the outcome, or exposes an auditor to influence or pressure which is prejudicial to their independence in any of its various facets; or whether such involvement would lead any person interested in the audit to believe that the auditor's independence was compromised or would be damaging to the authority of the auditor in the opinion of any such person.

Other work for the same organisation. Independence may be impaired where the other work is performed for the same organisation as is subject to audit and involves association with the directors, managers or administrators of the organisation and a sharing of the commitment to the attainment of their goals or objectives, such as, for example, in management consultancy and advisory services or taxation advisory and negotiation services, rather than investigation and evaluation of their conduct, performance or achievement. The auditors may become unduly sympathetic to a directorial or managerial attitude or interpretation of events, or the work may involve the creation of systems and information rather than assessing the adequacy of the systems and information which have been created by the directors or managers. Equally important, auditors may be perceived by those to whom they report to have become too closely associated with the organisation and its directors, and so to have compromised their independence.

It is important to emphasise that it is not suggested that the situation between auditors and audited is one of conflict and confrontation, that auditors do not have a duty to understand the point of view of directors, managers or administrators, or that they can be wholly uninterested in the success of the organisation and the attainment of its goals. However, the primary reason for the existence of the audit obliges auditors to advise themselves, from the evidence, on the standard of conduct or performance of the persons audited. Any lack of rigour in seeking and examining the evidence or reporting thereon, occasioned by a predisposition in favour of the audited, would be damaging to the audit process.

If involvement in other work or if other association with the audited has the potential, consciously or unconsciously, to induce such a predisposition, or to lead others to believe that there is such a predisposition, then that involvement or association is prejudicial to audit independence.

Recommendations arising from the audit to remedy deficiencies in matters which are the subject of audit are obviously an extension of the audit report which cannot be regarded in any way as compromising audit independence. In the spectrum of professional services between these recommendations and management consultancy which advises on planning and policy, it is a question of fact when the service involves commitment which makes it objectionable.

The principle is that auditors cannot engage in services which potentially affect their mental attitude, impartiality and objectivity, and independence of thought and action, or which others might believe would so affect them. It is not proposed to attempt a discrete definition of auditing and related attest functions which would enable the proscription of all other services. It is the principle which is important for understanding. Application of the principle leaves little doubt that, as a generalisation, for the auditor of an organisation to give services to that organisation involving recommendations on policy is damaging to audit independence and to the appearance of audit independence; it will reduce the value of the audit and in some circumstances perhaps destroy it for the persons for whose benefit it is performed.

The issue is fairly straightforward where it is the position of an individual auditor which has to be considered. In most cases, however, particularly in public companies, public boards, etc., the auditor will be a firm, and the person who acts as auditor will not personally be responsible for all the other services, although they will be given in the name of the firm. In some cases, these services may be given by an associated firm of the same name. Whatever the organisational and constitutional structure, there is a potential conflict of interest which consciously or unconsciously puts pressure on independence of thought and action when the auditor has to consider whether to comment on or to take exception to something in which the firm has been involved in another capacity. It could also be the case, for example, that in evaluating a system of recording and processing transactions and of internal control an auditor places greater reliance on that system than would have been the case if there were not a predisposition to a favourable assessment because the firm in another capacity had been involved in its creation or development. The appearance of absolute independence is inevitably compromised by involvement in activities which must later be subjected to audit scrutiny. Where separate departments or firms carry on practice in the same or similar name, there must be some doubt as to whether the significance of the separation is appreciated by the user public and whether their perception of independence will be affected by the arrangement. It is also a moot point whether any potential impairment of independence can be totally eliminated when there remains an economic bond or a legal bond – particularly a bond of joint responsibility and liability. The loyalty and common understanding which exist between partners in the same firm and affiliated firms are persuasive forces which should not be discounted.

It is not suggested that the provision of other services to an audited organisation by the auditor requires to be proscribed. The proposition is that this has the potential for detracting from audit authority by its effect on independence or the appearance of independence, and that this must be a matter for consideration in each case. There can, of course, be a net benefit to the organisation by auditors bringing to the consultancy or other work the knowledge and experience obtained from acting as auditors. Any compromise of independence must, however, be avoided in organisations in which there is a public interest in accountability – public companies, public boards, governments, etc. In other organisations any loss of independence can only be acceptable if disclosed to and acquiesced in by the relevant groups to whom the auditor's report is addressed.

Other work for another organisation. Where the other work is performed for organisations other than those which are audited, there is no specific conflict of interest or improper pressure or influence in relation to the audited organisation. There is also no reason to suggest that involvement in non-audit services has the potential for prejudicing audit independence by inducing a mental attitude, the objectivity of which has been impaired, or that auditors would become unduly influenced by a general directorial or managerial point of view. Indeed, the experience of auditors with directors and managers in non-audit situations is likely to contribute to their audit competence.

A more difficult issue is whether such involvement by auditors affects the institutionalised projection of audit independence and so the users' perception of the independence of the auditor in any individual audit.

The institutionalised projection of independence is the generalised view which society forms from the way the conduct of auditors conforms to the perception of their role. 'Independence' is a definitive characteristic of audit as the social expectation has evolved. The experience of society of the conduct of auditors in different situations will be, or will not be, supportive to that expectation and perception dependent on the interpretation by user groups of the significance of how auditors do act. Absolute independence is an ideal concept, and every association has potential for detracting from it. If the involvement of auditors in non-audit services has the potential to affect the institutionalised projection of audit independence, it is a matter of fact whether the impact is of material significance.

The involvement of firms in consultancy and other work which is the subject of public controversy or which is politically sensitive gives the firms a public profile which may well have an effect on the institutional reputation of the auditing profession for independence and impartiality. The facts that the auditors as individuals are not involved and that the work is carried out and reported on to high professional standards in fulfilment of the terms of reference – which are likely to be directed to specific issues and are not the same as an audit – will not necessarily impress a public which is already sceptical about the general ethical concept of professional independence.

Auditor independence is not a natural concept immediately comprehended and accepted by the public: constant positive action is necessary to sustain it.

4.4 Review

Audit independence is a concept which is a constituent element of audit credibility and authority. It is achieved through the independence of auditors in their mental attitude, which governs their capacity for independent thought and action, impartiality and objectivity, in their organisational separation, and in their investigative and reporting freedoms.

Organisational arrangements and other related circumstances can create conditions which are supportive to the desired mental attitude and which lead others to believe in the independence of auditors. However, organisational arrangements and these other circumstances do not make auditors independent. Independence, as defined, is a personal matter for each auditor. There is no reason to believe that, provided there is freedom of investigation and reporting, an auditor cannot have the right mental attitude and act with independence in spite of unsatisfactory organisational arrangements and objectionable circumstances. However, in such a case, belief in that independence on the part of the user public is difficult to achieve because the auditor does not have the appearance of independence.

On the other hand, while ideal organisational arrangements and other circumstances remove obstacles to the achievement of independence, and support belief in that independence, they cannot guarantee that an auditor will investigate and report with impartiality and objectivity. The correct mental attitude, independent thought and action, impartiality and objectivity and use of freedom of investigation and reporting, are ultimately dependent on the personal qualities of the auditor. Belief in the authority of the audit which stems from independence is likewise dependent on the view which the user has of the personal qualities of the auditor.

The more remote the users are from the auditor and from the subject of audit, the more they must rely on the organisational arrangements, the public reputation of the auditor and the public perception of the auditing profession to reassure them as to the independence of the audit in a particular situation. If the users are close enough to the situation to make a personal assessment of the matter, they are less dependent on the organisational arrangements as a basis of confidence in the independence of the audit, although these are still relevant and important. It is for this reason that, although there is an ideal concept of audit independence and it is possible to identify those factors which are supportive of and those which are detrimental to its achievement, auditor independence is relative and not absolute.[2] There are degrees of independence, and the rigour of the test to be applied depends on the importance of the outcome, the element of public interest (as distinct from private interest) involved, and the remoteness of the users from the auditor.

The issues which are at stake are authority and user confidence. If the audit has sufficient authority for its intended purpose without absolute independence, or the appearance of it, or if any shortfall in absolute independence, or the appearance of it, is made good by the users by reassurance from another source, then the social purpose is being served. The social utility of an audit is not invalidated solely by reason of the fact that there is less than, or the appearance of less than, absolute independence.

In the case of audit of central government departments, local government, public boards, public listed companies (in the private sector) and similar organisations, the importance of the outcome, the element of public interest involved, and the remoteness combine to impose a requirement that the highest degree of auditor independence be demanded to produce the greatest possible expectation that an independent audit will be achieved and be seen to be achieved. In less public organisations such as the small private firm, while the auditor personally must still conform to standards of objectivity and impartiality, and there are 'arm's length' users interested in the audit – bankers, creditors, employees – the position may be distinguished. In establishing the credibility and authority of the audit based on its independence, personal assessment of the auditor's quality and capabilities is likely to be relatively more important than the rigour of the arrangements. Any shortcomings in the arrangements by reference to established criteria should, however, be disclosed.

In these cases, where there is some modification of the element of public interest, the remoteness and the importance of the outcome, consideration must be given to *all* the circumstances in coming to a view as to whether the organisational arrangements are appropriate. In a small private firm, for instance, where it is suggested that in normal circumstances some lack of rigour in the arrangements would not be detrimental to belief in the actuality of the independence of the audit, provided the deficiency in the arrangements is disclosed, the situation would be different if there were a clear conflict of interest between interested groups. A critical situation for creditors or lenders, conflict between groups of shareholders (an oppressed minority), or a demand for attestation of information for wage negotiation, could produce a situation in which greater rigour in the arrangements was essential to support belief in audit independence and the appearance of it.

Ethics 5

In addition to competence and independence, the authority of the audit is sustained by the status of auditing as a profession and by the ethical standards of auditors.

Public trust and confidence in auditors are dependent on a continuing belief in their unqualified integrity, objectivity, and, in appropriate circumstances, acceptance of a duty to the public interest, with a consequential subordination of self-interest. Creating and retaining trust and confidence, therefore, requires auditors to show certain characteristics, which are those commonly associated with employments which are recognised and sanctioned by society as professions.

The definition of a profession as a distinctive social occupational group is rarely attempted except by reference to empirically determined common features which are considered to be exhibited by employments regarded as professions. There does seem, however, to be a general understanding of what professions are and an acceptance that they do carry authority because of what they are. Auditing does require the authority which professionalism gives, and auditors must, therefore, exhibit those features which entitle them to recognition as a professional group.

5.1 Features of a Profession

The most essential features of an employment described as a profession are that:

1. Those engaged in that employment offer to members of the public services essential to the public (principally those which affect health, welfare, wealth and legal relationships, rights and interests) which require specialist knowledge and skill, intellectually based with a systematic theory and necessarily requiring an advanced level of education, training and experience to obtain competence.

2. Because of the special nature and complexity of the services, those untrained in them cannot competently judge their quality.

3. Because of the specialist nature of the services, the users' inability to judge their quality, and the users' need to be able to depend on them, in the interest of public protection a procedure is required for designating those persons who are 'qualified' to provide the services and can, therefore, be relied on – with the incidental consequence that the 'unqualified' are also thereby identified.

4. Because of the consequential public dependence on the honesty and integrity of the practitioners and the scope, therefore, for persons providing the services to take advantage of the public by serving their own self-interest, a commitment to objectivity, impartiality and service in the public interest is required of the practitioners.

5. Because of the public's dependence on the competence and proper conduct of the practitioners, a procedure is required to monitor the maintenance of standards of competence and behaviour, and to discipline unsatisfactory practitioners and in appropriate cases to exclude them from the 'qualified'.

5.2 Professional Regulation

It follows that admission to membership of a profession and recognition as being 'qualified' are synonymous, and that protection of the public requires prescription of the conditions on which that status is achieved. Arrangements must therefore be made for regulation of the professional group and

1. To specify the education, training and experience required for admission to the profession;

2. To specify the conditions of competence, conduct and otherwise under which membership of the profession may be continued or discontinued;

3. To stipulate how those who have satisfied the prescribed conditions for membership of the profession may be identified by the public;

4. To specify the particular circumstances in which provision of the services should be restricted to those persons who are designated as 'qualified'.

This can either be organised by the state or by a society of practitioners to whom the state has delegated authority. This latter is described as self-regulation, and is the method used in the United Kingdom. Self-regulation has the advantage that it removes regulation from the risk of being subject to undesirable political influence. However, self-regulation carries with it the risk that unless carefully supervised it could degenerate into regulation for the protection of the practitioners rather than of the public.

Recognition of a *qualified* professional group becomes more necessary as the complexity of the services and their importance in the public interest increases. Designation of the qualified, i.e. the members of the profession, is intended for the protection of members of the public to enable them to make an informed choice. Professional regulation is also by its nature a protective measure for members of the profession, since it does restrict competition, particularly if there are a large number of designated protected functions, closed to the 'unqualified'.

Recognition of a professional group does not by itself prevent the engagement in the relevant services by non-members of the profession, except to the extent that specified functions are closed. Members of the public are free to engage the services of non-members but must make their own assessment of competence and reliability. Thus there is inevitably a competitive factor in favour of the professional group, even in the non-designated functions.

There is, therefore, an onus on the profession and on the regulating agency, public or private, to ensure that regulation is limited and directed to what is necessary to protect the public interest, is not extended beyond what is necessary for that purpose, and is not distorted as a restrictive practice for members of the profession.

5.3 Professional Conduct

The obligations of members of a profession to demonstrate honesty, integrity and a disinterested concern for the public interest impose on them standards of conduct if they are to continue to enjoy public trust and confidence, and the social protection and privilege with the status and economic benefit which recognition as 'qualified' confers.

There was a time when claims to membership of a profession were assumed to imply that the members accepted and professed a commitment to well-established and well-understood standards. It is now the case that for the information of the public, the guidance of members, and as a basis of regulation, a more formal approach has become necessary. Codes of ethics or ethical guidelines have been drawn up setting out the principles of professional conduct considered necessary to sustain public confidence in the professional virtues which are claimed.

The professional concept is not without its critics, and there is a good deal of scepticism about what is described as the professional ideal. The disinterested, altruistic objectives of professional regulation are discounted as unproven assertions; and, particularly in a self-regulatory system, exclusion of the uninitiated, control of entry, and the licensing of members are seen as cover for arrangements which have as their real objectives to control a market for particular services and to establish autonomy and control of the terms of work. This has to be countered, since the public interest demands in the provision of professional services those qualities which are the essence of what is embraced in the concept of professionalism.

5.4 The Auditing Profession

All this certainly holds in the case of auditing. Accountability is necessary for both public and private control. Auditing is necessary to secure accountability. Confidence of the public in audit authority and in the credibility and reliability of audit reporting requires on the part of auditors those qualities which are associated with professionalism.

In securing accountability, in reporting on the reliability and credibility of information in accounts and other statements, in expressing opinion on conduct and performance measured by reference to established norms, for their reports and opinions to have social value and to fulfil the needs and expectations of those persons for whose benefit and reassurance audits are carried out, auditors require to have established reputations for integrity, objectivity, impartiality and independence. They must be known to accept an overriding regard for the public interest, which is most material in organisations where accountability is of the greatest public concern, for example government, public boards and public listed companies, and to be prepared to subordinate self-interest. It is only if auditors exhibit this professionalism that the public can have a basis for confidence and trust in the capacity of the audit to fulfil its social function.

5.5 Ethical Guidelines

Ethics in its ordinary, unqualified usage refers to moral principles of human conduct. Professional ethics include social ethics but are not confined to them. A professional code of ethics is a set of rules or guidelines which are basic principles of correct action for members of a profession or conventions of professional conduct designed to protect the institutional reputation of professionalism, i.e. to promote adherence to the kind of conduct which the public interest requires.

Ethical guidelines are addressed to issues which confront

members of a profession in rendering their services, and prescribe the course of action which will be in the public interest in sustaining confidence and authority.

The overriding principle of the code of professional ethics designed to sustain the authority of auditors is that their conduct should be governed by the precepts of integrity, objectivity, impartiality, independence, regard for the public interest and subordination of self-interest, and by a concern not to do anything which would bring the profession into disrepute.

The principal matters which are generally dealt with in an ethical code are:

(a) professional competence
(b) professional independence and disqualifying circumstances and relationships
(c) confidentiality
(d) incompatible activities or occupations
(e) obtaining professional work, publicity and advertising.

Professional competence

The importance of professional competence has already been dealt with in Chapter 3. Lack of competence for any specific work undertaken is damaging to professional authority and reputation. The objective of an ethical guideline on the subject is to underline the public's expectation of relevant competence, and to emphasise the duty of auditors to maintain professional competence as required by changes in knowledge and practice, and the obligation of auditors not to accept a specific work assignment for which they do not have the requisite competence.

Professional independence

The importance of professional independence has already been dealt with in Chapter 4. Lack of independence or of the appearance of independence in an auditor in any particular circumstances is damaging to the auditor's professional authority and reputation. The objective of an ethical guideline on the subject is to emphasise the critical nature of independence in relation to audit authority and, as required by circumstances from time to time, to recommend appropriate action for situations which are likely to be damaging to independence and consequently to audit authority and professional reputation.

Confidentiality

Auditors have freedom of investigation and, accordingly, are entitled to receive such information and explanations as they consider to be necessary *for the purposes of the audit*. The auditor is the judge of the necessity and the information and explanations cannot unreasonably be withheld. As a result, auditors are possessed of much information of a highly sensitive (and in the case of individuals, personal) nature, the disclosure of which to any other person could be damaging, embarrassing or perhaps only undesirable as far as the audited are concerned. Auditors receive the information on the basis that it will be used only for the purposes of the audit. Auditors have a duty of confidentiality in relation to that information as a basis of trust and confidence in their integrity and, accordingly, as a basis of trust in the authority of the audit.

The objective of an ethical guideline is again to emphasise the importance of this matter and, if required from time to time, to identify particular circumstances for which a preferred course of action is recommended.

Incompatible activities or occupations

Reference has already been made in Chapter 4 to the relevance of conditions of operation affecting organisational status in establishing and maintaining audit independence and the appearance of independence. Audit authority is critically dependent on confidence in an auditor's integrity, objectivity, impartiality and freedom of thought and action in relation to the audit. Any activity or occupation which compromises or appears to compromise confidence in these characteristics is damaging to audit authority.

This is a matter of particular difficulty. Experienced and sound judgement which is sensitive to public reactions is needed to identify those activities which should be avoided. Changing public attitudes and new circumstances are likely to require review on a continuous basis and revision and modification from time to time of the recommended course of action.

The value of a guideline is to advise auditors authoritatively on what are perceived to be potential difficulties. Activities which may produce conflict of interest are obviously objectionable, and reference has already been made in Chapter 4 to certain consultancy work. Investment management also has the potential for conflict of interest. Ancillary activities such as agencies for products (e.g. computer software) or services (e.g. insurance) which would appear to be likely to militate against impartial evaluation are also objectionable. Commercial activities which appear to conflict with principles of objectivity and impartiality in their operation, or with concern for the public interest and subordination of self-interest are likely to appear to the public to be inconsistent with the institutional status and reputation of auditing. These are matters of judgement, and it is therefore important that auditors should observe the principle involved rather than only follow the ethical guidelines as if they were comprehensive and inflexible rules.

Obtaining professional work, publicity and advertising

These are probably the matters which raise the most difficult ethical issues. The primary objective of ethical constraints on auditors' conduct is to sustain public confidence in auditors and in their capacity for integrity, objectivity, impartiality and independence, commitment to the public interest and the subordination of self-interest. Auditors must refrain from any behaviour which militates against this.

The public, individuals and organisations, are expected to choose auditors on the basis of reputation: the regulation of entry, standards, disciplinary procedures, and professionalism should provide reassurance of expectations of competence. Soliciting and advertising for work and publicity directed towards attracting work have for long been regarded unfavourably as inconsistent with good professional behaviour. In one of the few contributions to the literature on ethics in the accountancy profession, Barradell (1969, p. 23) wrote: 'one feature which such generally accepted professions as accountancy, medicine, and the law all have in common is the prohibition of all forms of advertising, solicitation or touting for professional business'. That was less than twenty years ago, but the precept could not be written in such uncompromising and unambiguous terms today. That was the philosophy which was spelt out in ethical guidelines, but they contained some inherent inconsistencies which has led to the modification of the guidance which has been made in the intervening period.

While there can be nothing objectionable in solely informational publicity in relation to professional services, which by definition are specialist in nature and in technicality beyond the understanding of the 'lay' user, self-promotion which claims or appears to claim superior skill may mislead the public and distort choice. The persuasive influence on selection may be the effectiveness of the promotion rather than the personal professional reputation of the individual or firm. There can be no reason why a person or firm should not take steps to make it generally known that they are professionally qualified to audit; to go beyond that and claim or imply superior skill or better service or some other superiority over other auditors, which cannot be substantiated or verified by the public, is not in the public interest. If challenged, it places the reputation for integrity at risk; and self-promotion is liable to sit uneasily with a reputation for the subordination of self-interest.

The public must have some basis on which to judge. Reputations are achieved by demonstrating professional skills in practice; in addition, engagement in activities which provide the public with an opportunity to make personal assessments is quite proper. However, the concept of commercial marketing of auditing services, particularly if 'high profile' and 'aggressive', is in contradiction with the principle of professional excellence being the primary criterion for attracting work. Regulation of entry and discipline, together with adherence to the precepts of professionalism and ethics, are designed to secure that auditors have a minimum competence for any appointments that they accept. Selection by the public should be on the perceived professional excellence or other attributes of character and personality which commend themselves to the selectors.

Any method of obtaining an audit appointment which compromises independence or the appearance of independence is objectionable; so too are any practices which may be thought to be damaging to the institutional reputation of the auditing profession or to bring it into disrepute. It is for this reason that solicitation, 'touting', any method of direct approach to a potential client may be regarded as in breach of the ethical standard expected of an auditor. Some security of appointment is necessary to protect the independence of auditors, and there is generally some provision to ensure that auditors cannot be removed till after they have reported; but effective auditing may require continuing appointment for a number of terms (subject to satisfactory performance) so that it is not in the longer-term interest of the public or of the auditing profession's authority for auditors to be over-active in efforts to displace present incumbents. This is, however, a restriction on competition, and it has to be justified in order to be a legitimate acceptable constraint. There is a danger that the practice operates as a mutual protection by creating conventional obstacles in the way of desirable opportunity for change.

Difficulties in these matters underline the importance of having a well-considered system for the appointment and remuneration of auditors which protects their independence and authority and recognises the necessity of representatives of all interested parties participating in the procedures.

Ethical guidelines should be directed to the preferred course of action which is recommended in the specified circumstances. In formulating the guidance it is the public interest which must determine the extent of constraint on freedom of competition which is imposed.

5.6   Monitoring, Supervision and Maintenance of Standards

In order to sustain public confidence and audit authority it is necessary that the regulatory agency should monitor the conduct of auditors and their professional standards. Circumstances will determine whether the monitoring system should be passive, reacting only to reported alleged defaults, or active, with the power and resources to investigate auditors' work and conduct on a systematic basis. The important matter is that it is an integral element of professional or 'qualified' recognition that failure to adhere to the standards of recognition should result in an auditor's position being reviewed. It is equally important that the system should be seen to be operating rigorously.

The disciplinary procedures operated by the regulatory agency, private or public, are an essential part of the arrangements for the maintenance of standards of practice, and the regulatory agency needs to have the power to impose penalties and, if thought fit, to withdraw recognition of a member. Cases may be complex, and the regulatory agency requires to be able to command the resources to undertake the necessary investigation to ascertain the facts in the case of an alleged default.

These disciplinary proceedings are, of course, separate and distinct from civil or criminal legal actions in cases of alleged negligence or fraud, and do not in any respects replace them.

Public expectation of satisfactory standards of competence and conduct will be reassured by the equitable and open application of the disciplinary procedures with judgements exercised in the public interest. A failure of the disciplinary procedures to be seen to be protecting the public, for example by their seeming to have a predisposition in favour of protection of the auditors (whatever the reality may be), will fuel natural scepticism about the disinterestedness of a profession and result in erosion of the auditors' authority. The informality and judgemental quality of an ethical code and the resultant difficulties of defining and proving default which the uninitiated do not understand, tend to support a public belief that it is not enforced for the benefit of the public with enthusiasm and rigour, and that professionals 'close ranks' for mutual support when attacked. Some provision requires, therefore, to be made for non-professional involvement in the disciplinary process in order to enhance its credibility and authority, and as a consequence the authority of the audit. As part of the measures to sustain the authority of the audit, therefore, the importance of the disciplinary procedures cannot be overemphasised.

Auditing is a social function with onerous public obligations and responsibilities: the recognition and designation of auditors impose public responsibilities on them but also confer privilege and protection. The form of organisation of the audit function must be such that only fit and proper persons should be designated as qualified to be entrusted with the work, and that persons so designated who fall short of the required standard should be immediately excluded. The privilege and protection which auditors enjoy will only continue to be granted by society where it is apparent that in return society enjoys the benefit provided by auditing which is socially relevant, rigorous and authoritative.

Process III

Introduction to Part III

The audit process is concerned with what auditors require to do to discharge their responsibility. What kind of investigation should be undertaken: in what extent, depth and scope? What information and records should be examined and for what purpose? What evidence should be sought and what weight should be given to different types of evidence? How much evidence is required? What conclusions may be drawn from the evidence? In what terms and to whom should the audit findings be reported?

The audit process is a systematic examination of the matters which are the subject of audit to find out the relevant facts to inform the mind of the auditor, and from which the auditor may deduce conclusions and exercise judgement to arrive at an opinion or report.

The nature of the examination carried out, the evidence required, the facts established, and the conclusions considered are dependent on the nature of the accountability and the relative objective of the audit in the particular circumstances. The audit objective dictates what should be examined and what evidence is required to enable the auditor to give the opinion or make the report in terms which meet the audit objective. In turn, what has been examined and the evidence that has been collected dictate what the auditor is able to say by way of report or opinion. Shortcomings in the examination which could be made or in the evidence which could be collected may result in a report or opinion that the audit objective cannot be met or cannot be met in full. An audit of economy and efficiency in government, for example, requires a different investigation, different evidence and the exercise of judgement on different issues by an auditor, compared with an audit with the objective of expressing an opinion on the view given by the annual accounts of a company.

In no case can an auditor express an opinion or make a report without making an investigation and obtaining evidence. In all audits the pattern of the process is the same, and consists in:

(a) identifying the objective of the audit;

(b) planning the investigation and specifying the evidence to be obtained;

(c) carrying out the investigation and collecting the evidence;

(d) evaluating the evidence – pertinent, competent, sufficient, persuasive;

(e) proceeding to conclusions from the evidence – rational deduction, calculation, comparison;

(f) exercising judgement on the information that has been obtained;

(g) formulating the report or opinion.

These elements make up the three distinct stages of the audit process:

1. Obtaining, evaluating and drawing conclusions from the evidence.

2. Exercising judgement.

3. Reporting.

Audit practices and procedures are directed to the end of assembling the evidence which will inform auditors on those matters on which they must exercise judgement in order to report, for without evidence there can be no audit.

The concept and definition of what constitutes audit evidence, what Mautz and Sharaf (1961, p. 68) describe as 'competent evidential matter', and the principles governing use of that evidence by the auditor, are so vital as to be central elements in any theoretical structure for auditing. It is necessary, therefore, to address the following questions: What constitutes audit evidence? What are the criteria for the evaluation of audit evidence? How much and what kind of evidence is necessary to support an audit opinion or report? What is the relationship between evidence and auditor confidence?

There may not be wholly satisfactory answers to all of these questions, but clearly they have to be considered since audit practice and audit reports presume that there are answers; otherwise audit would be impossible.

The final stage in the audit process is communication in writing of the auditors' opinion or report. The terms of this are crucial, since auditors must convey completely, concisely and unambiguously the outcome of what is in many cases an extensive and complex investigation. The terms must be such that the persons to whom the opinion or report is addressed can understand the quality and extent of reassurance which an attestation provides, or the respects in which and the degree to which conduct, performance or achievement has compared with the standard of expectation – for example, in achieving economy or efficiency. They must be such that these persons can understand precisely in what respects the conduct, performance or achievement has fallen short of the standard.

The auditors' responsibility is to enable the persons to whom a report is addressed to make informed decisions and to take relevant action on the basis of those decisions. The auditors' role is that of faithful and impartial reporter, and the report, therefore, must be without bias or partiality to any interest. There are potential consequences for the parties who are audited. The impartial quality of the report is important to them in their belief in the integrity of auditors and their acceptance of the credibility of the auditors' judgement – although they might not necessarily agree with them. The terms of the audit report are therefore important to the maintenance of the authority of the audit as well as to the discharge of its social function.

Evidence

6

6.1 Basic Postulates

Three of the basic postulates set out in Chapter 2 are relevant to a consideration of the theory of audit evidence. The first is fundamental, and states the essential premise that without evidence an auditor has no basis on which to make a judgement, form an opinion or give a report:

The subject matter of audit, for example conduct, performance or achievement, or record of events or state of affairs, or a statement or facts relating to any of these, is susceptible to verification by evidence.

If the subject matter is not susceptible to verification by evidence because it is a matter for which no 'evidence' as required for audit exists, then there cannot be an audit. After investigation an auditor could only report that due to lack of verifiability no audit opinion or report can be made.

If the subject matter of the audit is verifiable but the audit evidence no longer exists or cannot be obtained, a similar consequence follows: an audit opinion or report would be impossible.

The second postulate which is relevant is that:

Standards of accountability, for example of conduct,

performance, achievement and quality of information, can be set for those who are accountable; actual conduct, performance, achievement, quality and so on can be measured and compared with those standards by reference to known criteria . . .

This proposition underlies the basis of the specific criteria which auditors must establish to decide what evidence must be obtained to enable the audit opinion or report to be prepared to fulfil the audit function. Auditors must carry out such investigation and obtain such evidence as will enable them to measure and compare the relevant conduct, performance, achievement or quality with standards which are explicit or implicit in the audit terms of reference. Recognised standards must, accordingly, have been set and auditors must know what they are.

Finally, the postulate that

An audit produces an economic or social benefit

imposes a restriction on evidence which may be obtained where the economic and social cost of obtaining it exceed the economic and social benefit, with a resultant net cost or negative benefit. It is this constraint which requires auditors to consider alternative sources of evidence, which is an important factor in developing an audit plan, executing it and, if necessary, modifying it as the result of experience during its execution. It also requires auditors to distinguish between what is essential and what would be no more than interesting or desirable.

Time and cost are important, and the postulate means that auditors must apply this rigorous test in order to be satisfied that the additional assurance obtained is justified by the time and cost which will be incurred by obtaining the additional evidence. It also means that auditors must consider whether there are alternative sources of evidence which would provide the same or sufficient reassurance. Mautz and Sharaf (1961) discuss this matter and conclude:

time may not permit the auditor to take the necessary steps to obtain compelling evidence, *even if it is available* [emphasis added] . . . [And] it would be unreasonable to incur substantial costs to ascertain the existence of assets of inconsequential

amounts. It might also be unreasonable to incur substantial costs to prove the existence of assets of even significant amounts if other types of evidence are sufficiently persuasive and more readily available. The difference between compelling evidence and very persuasive evidence may not be sufficiently important to warrant the added cost of obtaining the former. On the other hand, other things being equal, compelling evidence is much the more desirable. (Mautz and Sharaf, 1961, pp. 84–5)

6.2 Competent Evidence

Obtaining the relevant competent evidence is the central purpose of the audit investigation process. If the available evidence is limited, deficient or inadequate, the auditors' opinion or report will as a consequence be circumscribed, restricted or qualified by reference to the shortcomings. The quality of the evidence and extent of it determine the terms of an auditor's opinion or report so that a vitally important task for auditors is to assess the meaning, significance and persuasiveness of evidence for the issue to which it relates. The level of confidence which auditors have about a particular matter is dependent on their assessment of the evidence which is available to support it. The interaction and interdependence between evidence and responsibility are the crucial factors in determining both the programme of investigation and the terms of the report. In explanation of his 'Theory of Inspired Confidence', Limperg (1985, first published 1932/3) explains an auditor's dual responsibility in the following terms:

> If the function is to achieve its objective, then no more confidence may be placed in its fulfilment than is justified by the work carried out and by the competence of the accountant, while conversely, the function must be fulfilled in a manner that justifies the confidence placed in its fulfilment.
>
> The normative core of the *Theory of Inspired Confidence* is therefore this: the accountant is obliged to carry out his work in such a way that he does not betray the expectations which he evokes in the sensible layman; and, conversely, the accountant may not arouse greater expectations than can be justified by the work done. This simple maxim applies independently of the

tenor of the expectations; whether these are extensive or modest, the community may never be disappointed in its expectations. In its normative core, the Theory does not lay down definite rules about what the accountant has to do in each particular case; that decision it leaves to him as a professional. But, as a guide for that decision, it gives him this general prescription, based on the consideration that the effective tenor of the function, thus its operation in the community, is determined by the confidence it inspires. In consequence, the Theory expects from the accountant that in each special case he ascertains what expectations he arouses; that he realises the tenor of the confidence that he inspires with the fulfilment of each specific function. To that end, it is necessary that he has an insight into the factors that determine the substance of that confidence. (Limperg, 1985, pp. 17 and 19)

An auditor's responsibility is almost invariably the expression of an opinion, whether with a prescribed content such as in an auditor's report on annual accounts, or with content specially related to the circumstances, as in an auditor's report on a management audit. As a general rule auditors do not certify, do not guarantee, and are not seeking certainty. Auditors are not seeking evidence to *prove* anything: they are seeking sufficient evidence which not only provides the basis for their opinion or report, but which also gives them the level of confidence which satisfies the needs and expectations of those persons who seek the benefit of the audit. What is sought from an auditor is an expert professional opinion. Evidence provides the rational grounds for that opinion. Since it is a professional opinion that is sought, it is ultimately a matter of personal judgement for auditors to decide what they understand the evidence to mean and whether they have sufficient evidence to form an opinion or prepare a report. An auditor's opinion is an expert opinion, and it is, therefore, based on knowledge, training and experience in auditing. There is a framework within which auditors exercise their own judgement and there are professional standards to which they must have regard in reaching their opinion. There must, therefore, be a basis for scrutiny of evidence against some criteria, evaluating it, and deciding the conclusions which can be drawn from it. The theory of audit evidence is concerned with what that basis and those criteria are, and the logical links between the evidence and the conclusions.[1]

It is the effect of the evidence on the mind of the auditor that matters, and whether that evidence takes the auditor to a sufficient state of confidence about the issues to be considered so that the report will convey the benefit which the audit is designed to achieve. Anything with a bearing on the issue which has the potential for having an influence on the mind of the auditor must, therefore, be considered for its evidential quality. It is for that reason that an auditor is interested in oral testimony, written testimony, physical productions, deductive reasoning, inference and probability. Each of these types of evidence has limitations in varying degrees of persuasiveness. The auditor has to assess the persuasiveness of the evidence as regards the subject matter and in relation to the confidence which the auditor wishes to have.

The persuasive quality of the evidence will depend on its intrinsic nature and the reliability of its source. For example, oral and written testimony originated under the control of the persons audited does not have the same quality as independent evidence originated by disinterested third parties. Written testimony from an apparently independent source is of limited value without some assurance as to its authenticity and the care and diligence with which it has been prepared. Evidence cannot be accepted at its face value.

There may be evidence from more than one source bearing on the subject of enquiry, two or more of oral, written, and physical evidence and deductive reasoning about the same matter – and each is likely to have different degrees of persuasiveness. Each piece of evidence on its own may be of limited value and insufficient for the audit purpose, but evidence of a varied nature from different sources all bearing on the same matter has a cumulative effect, and accordingly, it is this which auditors must evaluate.

While different audits require different investigations and the collection of different evidence to inform the auditor on the subject of the audit, the process is essentially the same. Without sufficient evidence of actual events and actions related to the subject of audit auditors cannot form an opinion on, for example, the adequacy and integrity of accounting records – absence of error, misrepresentation, deceit, dishonesty and fraud;

the information given by an accounting statement (the financial position is fairly presented, or in accordance with law, or that a true and fair view of the state of affairs is given);

the economy and/or efficiency of the administration of departments of government in the implementation of policies, for example, in health, education or defence;

the effectiveness of government policies in achieving defined objectives;

the standard of the several functional areas of management in a business (management audit);

the extent of adherence to internal controls and policies and of success in achieving policy goals (operational audit).

.3 Planning, Collecting and Evaluating Evidence

'he process of planning the investigation and collecting and valuating evidence in the case of a recurring audit with a onsistent terms of reference, such as the annual audit of company ccounts, may be more structured and the pattern, if not the etail, more standardised than in some other audits, but in rinciple all audits are the same. The process requires:

a) identifying the objective of the audit;

b) planning the investigation and specifying the evidence to be obtained;

) carrying out the investigation and collecting the evidence;

d) evaluating the evidence – pertinent, competent, sufficient, persuasive;

e) proceeding to conclusions from the evidence – rational deduction, calculation, comparison;

) exercising judgement on the information that has been obtained;

g) formulating the report or opinion.

The audit enquiry is directed towards the relevant evidence. The evidence that is relevant will, of course, depend on the subject of the audit and the audit objective; and the sources and nature of the evidence will vary, as will the professional knowledge, skill and experience required to evaluate and use it. The issues that arise, however, are of general applicability, although in the various circumstances some may be more important than others.

In relation to the detection of error, irregularity and dishonesty in the management and the recording of the use of money and other resources, the relevant evidence which is sought depends on the level of responsibility of the auditor. In all organisations executive management have the primary responsibility for making arrangements to secure the safe custody of resources and the integrity of records and information. Internal auditors are concerned with verifying in detail that these arrangements are adhered to, that they are effective, and that deviations are rectified and dealt with. The responsibility of external auditors may vary, but as a general rule it has three elements. External auditors are required to consider whether the executive management have satisfactorily discharged their responsibility by the arrangements which they have made. The auditors must then consider, in the context of these arrangements, the possibility and probability of material error, irregularity and dishonesty taking place and remaining undetected or uncorrected, and, in relation to the audit objective and their responsibility, the significance of any error, irregularity, fraud, or other dishonesty that has taken place. However, they also have the more onerous responsibility of considering the possibility and probability of irregularity dishonesty and fraud on the part of executive management and non-executive board or committee members, and the significance of the incidence of any of these.

The standards of performance and the criteria for their evaluation are fairly straightforward in relation to error irregularity, dishonesty and fraud. It is essential, however, that the level of audit responsibility is defined to enable the evidence which must be obtained to be prescribed. The judgemental issue which is fraught with difficulty in establishing criteria of measurement is defining the degrees of materiality of departure from the standard in relation to the audit objective. This matter is considered in Chapter 8.

Where the audit objective is to express an opinion on, or to attest the information given by, a financial statement or set of accounts auditors must first of all be satisfied on the evidence as to the reliability of the data on which the statement or accounts have been prepared. As regards the statement or accounts, the evidence necessary to enable auditors to form an opinion on their content depends on the standard to which they have to conform. For example, this may be compliance with the requirements of an Act with respect to form and content, and giving a true and fair view of state of affairs and profit or loss (Companies Act 1985), or preparation in accordance with regulations and in observance of proper accounting practices and compliance with the requirements of applicable enactments and instruments (Local Government (Scotland) Act 1973). The evidence that is necessary to confirm compliance with the statutory prescription of detail in relation to the quality of information can be readily established, but the judgemental character of the concepts of 'a true and fair view' and 'proper accounting practices' gives rise to more difficulty. It is essential, however, that their meanings and the criteria for their evaluation should be well understood for it to be determined what evidence should be sought by an auditor. In this case also issues of materiality require to be considered.

The greatest difficulty arises, however, in those audits where the performance to be assessed is less readily susceptible to precise specification, for example economy, efficiency, effectiveness and managerial performance. There are problems of determining appropriate performance measures, and of using them to establish the norms of expectation and to assess actual performance. Accordingly, in cases where there are no well-established and accepted standards and criteria, it is imperative that the standards and criteria it is proposed to apply are specified in advance of the conduct of the audit, so that the relevant evidence may be obtained.

As a general proposition it may be said that there are few situations in which auditors make an exhaustive, comprehensive and total verification of the subject matter of an audit by reference to evidence. Even if that were possible and it were necessary to do it, auditors could not be completely confident, without reservation, that the matters verified had been proved, or that all the relevant information had been disclosed and that only the relevant information had been included and verified. Auditors do not verify at the time when the activity, event or transaction takes place and are dependent on evidence after the event for their knowledge of what actually happened. There is, therefore, always room for innocent or deceitful misrepresentation of what did happen.

6.4 Audit Risk

There are also few situations in which auditors need to make a total verification to give them sufficient information and sufficient confidence to give an audit opinion or make a report which fulfils the audit objective. The cost-benefit test precludes auditors from continuing verification beyond the stage at which they have enough information and confidence to proceed to an opinion or report. Auditors can never be 100 per cent certain of the information on which their opinion or report is based. They must always proceed to an opinion in a situation of relative uncertainty. There is always a residual risk that because of the constraints of time, cost or practicability, evidence is not obtained which if it had been available would have made a difference to the auditor's opinion or report. This is in the nature of auditing and is a feature which those who use an audit must understand and accept. Further reference will be made to this later.

The result of this is that auditors must make a judgement as to the acceptable residual risk – that is, acceptable to the users – and as to the information and confidence which they require in the context of the audit objective. On these bases auditors must decide how much and what evidence should be sought, bearing in mind the synergism of evidence from different sources and the obligation to minimise the economic and social cost. Audit investigation and the collection and evaluation of evidence are, accordingly, almost invariably on a selective basis. The nature of the sample, the size of the sample and the persuasive evidential quality of the sample are matters which an auditor must decide. Once it is recognised that auditors cannot be 100 per cent certain, and that constraints of time, cost and practicability limit the evidence that can be obtained, it can be appreciated that not only are auditors expressing a personal professional opinion but also that that opinion is based on judgements and probabilities as to the underlying facts and circumstances. The more important the matter is in relation to an auditor's opinion and the audit objective, the more persuasive the evidence and the higher the degree of probability will require to be. In some cases only compelling evidence will be good enough.

6.5 Evaluation of Evidence

Auditors need to have considerable investigatory skill to evaluate audit evidence. Oral evidence and personal observation have a significant part in informing an auditor and influencing auditor judgement and confidence, but clearly they have a high degree of subjectivity and scope for misunderstanding. They may convey incomplete information. Oral evidence, in particular, may convey wrong information because of ignorance, misunderstanding or intent to deceive on the part of the informant; and an auditor's understanding of what is observed or intended to be conveyed may be at fault. Auditors' questions must be framed and observations designed to minimise these defects. A judgement on the honesty and credibility of the informant must be made, and the results of collateral questions and observations may also be used to enable an evaluation of the persuasive quality of such evidence.

Written evidence, consisting, for example, of documents, accounting and other records of transactions and events, periodic statements of results or performance, records of decisions, formal minutes, control records, internal memoranda and reports, has the appearance of greater objectivity and credibility particularly if initiated externally and/or is part of a system's information in which there are tests of internal consistency and intrinsic correctness. However, written evidence can be fabricated, falsified or interfered with innocently or with intent to deceive, and auditors require to be satisfied as to its authenticity and reliability. This requires making a judgement as to the independence, integrity and reliability of the source, the effectiveness of the control over what is originated, and the security of the arrangements for custody of the written or recorded material.

Deductive reasoning is by far the most important and also the most difficult source of audit evidence. It includes system evaluation, analytical review, the judgemental conclusions from the results of sampling, recognising and using the logical relationships of connected events, transactions, facts and consequences, and appreciating the relevance of changing conditions. It also includes judging the reasonableness and validity of the propositions which are the subject of audit and the opinion about them which is forming in the auditor's mind in the context and circumstances of the known internal and external environment. It is an intellectual process, and includes not only the application of the processes of logical deduction to all aspects of the propositions which are the subject of audit, but also the apparently inspirational element in audit enquiry by which the mind of an experienced auditor develops acute sensitivity to recognition of the abnormal or unexpected which is highly relevant to an opinion on the audited propositions.

System evaluation is an important source of evidence for auditors in forming an opinion on the probability, possibility and incidence of error, irregularity, dishonesty and fraud, and on the credibility and verifiability of data and information produced by the system. Where a system of accounting and internal control has been well designed and adhered to in operation, and its integrity secured by effective internal check and internal audit, a high degree of reliability may be placed on the data derived from the system. Once auditors have satisfied themselves by inspection that there is a high degree of probability that this is the case, the system constitutes highly persuasive audit evidence. A system must, however, be tested by an auditor to establish the extent to which it can be relied on, and to identify points where it is vulnerable and for which other evidence must be obtained. There will always be some matters which are so important in relation to the audit objective and the auditors' confidence of the basis of their opinion or report, that substantive evidence bearing directly on the matters will be required.

Computerised information systems produce particular problems of security and control, to ensure the reliability of the system and to protect the integrity of the data, but the principle is unchanged. If the system is vulnerable due to inadequate controls, its evidential value is limited, no matter how efficient it is in processing and outputting data. If a system cannot be relied on, auditors must seek other evidence to establish the authenticity of the output.

Where audit investigation and the collection and evaluation of evidence are on a selective basis, the sample size, method of selection and interpretation of results may be on either a judgemental or a statistical basis. In the first case the selection criteria are based on the subjective judgement of the auditor derived from experience and knowledge of the general practice of the profession. Statistical sampling reduces but does not eliminate the use of auditor judgement. An auditor must still personally decide for the population being sampled an acceptable error rate, the precision limit, and the confidence level required. Statistical sampling does, however, enable mathematical measurement of the confidence that may be obtained and the uncertainty that remains as a result of a partial examination. In some circumstances this focuses the issue for auditor judgement and assists in evaluation of the audit risk. There remains the difficulty of assessing subjectively the extent to which the statistical uncertainty is overcome by the judgemental evaluation of evidence from other sources as the result of the synergism proposition referred to above.

The results of systematic and analytical review, and the knowledge obtained from the application of skilled and experienced judgement to the particular facts and circumstances of an audit in the context of the current internal and external environment, are crucial parts of the total sum of evidence on which an auditor's report or opinion is finally based. In every profession, in addition to a high degree of advanced knowledge, skill and experience, there is an element of art and inspiration. These qualities have an indispensable and invaluable part to play in identifying the uniquely relevant evidence which an auditor should look for in the final analytical and judgemental review in the process of formulating an audit opinion or report.

Reporting 7

The final stage of the audit process is a communication by an auditor to those persons who have a legitimate interest in the audit and in the accountability of those whose conduct, performance, achievement, information, accounts or report has been the subject of audit examination.

The audit investigative process is extensive, detailed and complex, and requires special professional skill derived from education, training and experience. The responsibility of auditors is to convey to persons who do not have direct access to the relevant data and who do not have special knowledge of the peculiar technicality of auditing, the nature and extent of the reassurance they can give about information these persons already have, or to convey to them information which they wish to have with an evaluation of it to enable them to take appropriate decisions and action on some aspects of accountability or on some failure to adhere to the standard of expectation. In the first case this could be, for example, the attestation of accounts, lending credibility to the information which they purport to give; in the second case, it could involve expressing an opinion on honesty, regularity, economy, efficiency or effectiveness, or reporting the incidence of fraud, maladministration or managerial incompetence, or failure to observe procedures or attain goals.

7.1 Report Criteria

Overriding principles

Audit reports have potentially serious consequences for all parties involved. The inadequacy of a report and the failure to communicate successfully could result in consequences which were not justified by the facts, with injustice and damage to the interests of the parties.

In the remainder of this chapter where the context allows, 'report' will be used to imply opinion or report, including a relatively brief statement of opinion as in a company audit and the extensive reports which may be prepared in management audit.

Auditors are rarely in a position to engage in a dialogue with the parties who will use their report, and once released the report is frequently public information. Whatever it is that auditors have to communicate must be contained within the report issued at the completion of the audit. For all these reasons clarity and precision of language are overriding principles to be observed in expressing an opinion, particularly when there are qualifications or reservations in the opinion, and in formulating a report. This is especially so when allegations are made of criminal offences, serious failures, or incompetence.

Completeness of the report, exhaustion of the terms of reference, and explicit specification of matters of concern to the recipient are essential. It is many years since an English judge enunciated the dictum, in relation to an audit report on a financial statement, that

> **a person whose duty it is to convey information to others does not discharge that duty by simply giving them so much information as is calculated to induce them, or some of them, to ask for more. Information and means of information are by no means equivalent terms . . . an auditor who gives shareholders means of information instead of information in respect of a company's financial position does so at his peril, and runs the very serious risk of being held judicially, to have failed to have discharged his duty.**[1]

This principle, although formulated in a particular situation and in relation to the annual accounts of a company, is one of universal relevance. An audit report must be complete and explicit so that the reader at any time in the future knows fully and exactly what the auditors had to communicate as the outcome of the audit. It must be complete within itself, not requiring the reader to refer to any other document to understand its terms.

Auditors have been accused, if not of obfuscation, at least of incomprehensible technicality in the use of language, and it has been suggested by Inspectors in a Department of Trade investigation in the United Kingdom that

> **the sparse terminology employed by auditors has reached a stage of evolution when it may be described as hieratic. Such language may undergo a further stage of evolution as it frequently does in the law, when a phrase becomes a 'term of art' conveying to a lawyer a precise meaning which is quite different from its apparent meaning to a layman. Hieratic language suffers from every possible deficiency, being neither comprehensible as ordinary speech, nor adequately defined to a specialist.[2]**

Professional and technical precision

There is a serious dilemma for auditors. They have a duty to communicate and they have an obligation to be explicit and precise. This is equally important whether conveying reassurance or expressing criticism. The matters which are the subject of audit are frequently complex and highly specialised, and auditing itself is an advanced professional specialism. Auditors face the dilemma that they must communicate effectively with persons with limited or no technical understanding and at the same time must express themselves with sufficient technical precision to define precisely the terms and limits of the responsibility they undertake. The various groups of interested parties have different degrees of technical understanding, and in situations in which professional performance, diligence and competence are being judged in a court of law or other tribunal the terms of an audit report are liable to be subject to the most rigorous technical scrutiny.

There is an almost irreconcilable conflict between simplicity and professional, technical explication. Auditors must satisfy their professional obligations, but in doing so must try to be understandable as far as possible to the least knowledgeable of the potential legitimate interested parties.

Understandability

The range of capacity for understanding of potential users is widest in the case of the audit report on the accounts of a public listed company. However desirable it may be, it is unrealistic both in theory and in practice to expect an audit report which discharges an auditor's professional obligations to be understandable to the least knowledgeable of the recipients. Those who cannot comprehend all that it expresses and implies may take comfort from its being there, but they must rely on the more knowledgeable to alert them and, if necessary, to take action if an auditor reports matters of concern.

The existence of the audit, which is confirmed by the issue of an auditor's report, is an essential element in the social process of securing accountability and an indispensable contributory factor for continuing trust in the capital market system. For a great number of less knowledgeable users their confidence and reassurance is derived from their *belief* in the effectiveness of the audit rather than from their understanding of the audit process itself. For their faith to be justified the audit report must be in terms which enable the knowledgeable to be informed whether or not the duty of accountability has been satisfactorily discharged, whether or not accounts, reports or other statements provide the information which they should, and in what respects, if any, there have been failures or defaults or any description in relation to matters with which the recipients of the audit report are concerned.

The matters dealt with in the audit of companies are varied and difficult, requiring the use of substantial resources of skilled staff over a very considerable period of time. But particularly in the case of major public listed companies, and especially so in international groups, the audit examination is vastly extensive in scale and scope and highly complex in its nature. It has to be considered whether the outcome of this very elaborate enquiry and review can be effectively communicated in the few short sentences which generally constitute the auditor's report of a company or corporation.

The policy that has been pursued has been to shorten the satisfactory report as far as possible, generally with the objective that qualifications, reservations and amplifications will stand out and catch attention. The range and depth of the matters embraced in the auditor's report are implicit on the basis that readers understand what is comprised in an audit and that no comment means a satisfactory state of affairs. Whether this is in principle an adequate discharge of an auditor's reporting responsibility must be a matter of argument. The management letter to the board of directors in the United Kingdom, the longer form report to the board of directors in the USA, and even the report to the supervisory board in some European countries, do not meet the situation. The brief audit report, in the sense that it implies much more than it explicitly expresses, is something of a symbol or seal of approval of matters of which the standards, criteria and performance measures are by no means explicit, well-established and widely understood.[3]

The danger is that users' expectations exceed the responsibility which auditors can undertake on the basis of the work done, and that the report does nothing to correct such a misunderstanding. The evidence which exists of public misunderstanding of the audit function and of an 'expectation gap' to which reference was made in Chapter 1 suggests that such a danger is very real.

The principle is clear enough. An audit report should be clear, unambiguous and comprehensive in its disposal of the terms of reference. In 1932/3 Limperg (1985) expressed the philosophy simply in the terms already referred to in the Theory of Inspired Confidence. An auditor should not arouse greater expectation than can be justified by the work done. While it is also part of the Theory that auditors should endeavour to meet reasonable public expectations and audit is continually evolving, the terms of reference are established at any one time and auditors must take care that the extent of the responsibility which they undertake is clearly understood.

As far as audits other than those which relate to the preparation of accounts are concerned, the capacity for understanding of potential users varies. The diversity of the terms of reference and the need to make these clear as a preamble to reporting, and the terms of the report itself which will generally be specific to the particular case, should ordinarily ensure that there is no room for misunderstanding by those with a sufficient minimum knowledge to comprehend the issues involved. In such cases as the audit reports on economy, efficiency, effectiveness and operational and managerial performance, the performance measures that are used and the criteria for comparison with the norms adopted should be expressly stated and explained to establish confidence with the parties involved and to achieve successful communication of the meaning and significance of the audit evaluation. The precepts, of course, remain the same: clarity, precision, unambiguity and comprehensiveness in disposal of the terms of reference.

7.2 Report Details

In addition to the substantive part of the audit report, the matters which require to be included, unless there is good reason for not doing so, are:

1. Identification

    (a) of the parties addressed;

    (b) of the organisation to which the opinion or report refers;

    (c) of the accounts, statements or other matters to which the opinion or report refers.

2. Terms of reference.

3. Scope of examination.

4. Dating of the opinion or report.

5. Signature and designation of the auditor.

There may be cases where one or more of these matters may be thought to be self-evident or sufficiently well-established that knowledge of them may be assumed. In the interests of clarity and to avoid ambiguity or uncertainty, however, it is generally desirable that they should be explicit. They should certainly always be considered.

Identification of the parties addressed

This is necessary to establish to whom an auditor accepts primary responsibility. It puts other parties on notice that it was not their interests which the auditor had in mind in auditing and reporting, and that the report should be interpreted in that context. This may affect not only the scope of the audit and the report but also the extent to which the other users may rely on it. It may also affect the limit of any redress in law in the event of any damage to other users' interests as a result of their reliance.

Identification of the organisation (or part of the organisation) to which the report refers

The purpose of this is to make clear what organisation (or part of it) is the subject of the audit and to preclude the innocent or deceitful association of the report with an organisation to which it does not refer.

Identification of the accounts, statements or other matters to which the report refers

The purpose of this is to define the scope of the audit report. Particularly in the case of an opinion on accounts or financial statements, it is essential to identify positively and directly those accounts or statements that are embraced by the opinion. This explicitly excludes other accounts or statements which are related to and which may be attached to the audited ones. It also precludes the innocent or deceitful association of unaudited statements with the audit opinion, or extraction of parts of the audited statements so that the information given by the statements as a whole on which the audit opinion was based is materially affected.

Terms of reference

The terms of reference understood by the auditor should be

stated unless they are well established and tacitly understood or included in some other part of the audit report. This is the basis of the contract between the auditor and those for whose use the audit report is prepared; it is the premise from which the report has been derived. Understanding the audit report requires an understanding of the terms of reference, so it is essential that there is a mutual understanding between the auditor and the other parties involved.

Scope of examination

Information on the scope of the audit examination – its nature and extent – assists the user in forming an opinion as to the authority of the report and its usefulness for the decision or action which is contemplated. The scope may be explained positively or by exclusion and exception, so that the user has a general understanding of the basis on which the report has been prepared and in particular what has not been done. The facts that verification are on a selective basis and there is a residual audit risk (see Chapters 6 and 8) are significant to the users who may otherwise perceive the audit conclusions in more determinate terms. A reference to adherence to approved auditing standards may not convey much positive information to the uninitiated, but it does commit the auditor to a certain standard of performance and gives some reassurance to the user that the scope is consistent with general practice.

In the audit of economy, efficiency, effectiveness and operational and managerial performance a more specific and explicit description of scope is desirable as the basis of understanding and assessment of the conclusions of the audit report.

Dating of the report

This is the date on which the report is signed. It is important to establish the point of time up to which auditors could be expected to have knowledge of events and circumstances relevant to their report. This is particularly important for an opinion on accounts or financial statements involving a judgement on the outcome of uncompleted transactions and of future events affecting valuations. Events happening or information becoming available subsequent to that date may invalidate an opinion then formed. Auditors are expected to have informed themselves of all relevant matters up to the date of signing, and it is important to be able to establish at what date there was no means of knowledge of the further events or information which later had a material effect on the matters which were the subject of report.

Signature and designation of auditors

The audit report has no authority until signed, and auditors should confirm their authority by a description of their professional status. Auditors should understand that as a result of their professional status the fact alone of their signature lends authority to whatever it is associated. It is important, therefore, for them to ensure that it is precise and clear what their signature implies and that the message it conveys to the reader is no more than that for which they would be prepared to accept responsibility. The fact that persons of recognised integrity are prepared to be associated with some statements, activity or organisation could unwittingly give more reassurance to the public than the terms of their report, however carefully drawn, are intended to or do actually provide.

7.3 Publicity

The purpose of the audit report is to communicate to those persons who have a legitimate interest in the audit and in the accountability of the persons audited. It is essential, therefore, that there is unrestricted access to the report by the interested parties. In some cases there may be an obligation on the audited to distribute the report to some or all classes of interested parties; and in some cases the report is a matter of public record to which all members of the public have access. There are cases, however, where there is no clearly defined constituency to which the audited are accountable, and where there is no legal obligation to put the report on public record. In such cases the audit process is incomplete, and the social function of securing accountability has not been fulfilled unless appropriate publication of the audit report is undertaken.

In the case of government agencies, public boards, charities and other organisations with a duty of public accountability and where accountability is a matter of public concern, that duty is not discharged unless positive measures are taken to bring the audit report to the attention of the public.

Drawing attention to the significance of publicity in state audit, Normanton (1966, p. 155) observes: 'most of the examples of waste and extravagance, and of course all cases of fraud, are in some way reprehensible. If left to themselves, with no external audit, the authorities concerned would certainly not have drawn public attention to them.' Normanton quotes a statement by a member of the French Cour des Comptes: 'it is certainly useful that light, full light, is shed upon the conditions in which the taxes, which impose heavy sacrifices upon every citizen, are employed . . . light is the prerequisite of good order'.

Not only in the public sector but as adapted appropriately to the private sector, this is the guiding principle for the final stage of the audit process in its contribution to securing accountability and to social control. Full light is the prerequisite of good order.

Materiality

8

In the course of planning and executing an audit auditors require to make decisions on how to proceed, and to make choices among alternative courses of action. They must decide how to conduct the investigation, the scope, extent and depth of the examination, and the nature and volume of evidence to obtain. They must decide how to react, in what respects the investigation should be developed, and how earlier decisions on required evidence should be revised as a result of what they learn in the course of the planned investigation. Finally they must decide what should be contained in the opinion or report, or what other action, if any, they should take to discharge their responsibility on the basis of the information they have obtained.

All these decisions depend on how important in the mind of the auditors the matters are in relation to the audit objective and/or on how important they are to the auditors in informing themselves on the subject matter of their opinion or report. These decisions depend on what in auditing is described as the 'materiality' of the issue on which an auditor must take a decision. The meaning of materiality in the following discussion is wider than is commonly adopted in treatments of the subject, but is not in conflict with the narrower interpretation.[1]

Materiality in auditing is the characteristic which determines the nature, quality and quantity of evidence which auditors require about any matter or proposition. It is the materiality of any item which determines what evidence auditors require to take their mind to that state of confidence about any proposition which enables and entitles them to express an opinion or to report. Materiality is also the measure of the impact which any piece of information produced by the audit investigation has in stimulating further enquiry; or the value of information for the purposes of the report or opinion which an auditor proposes to make to discharge the audit responsibility and fulfil the audit purpose. It may be impact or value to the auditor in the sense of the effect on the mind of the auditor in relation to the audit objective and/or the content of the report. It may be value to the receivers of the report in relation to their decision.

The concept of materiality permeates the whole audit process. It is necessary, therefore, that its meaning and significance should be fully understood. For this purpose it is convenient to consider materiality in the three stages of the audit process:

1. Planning.

2. Execution: investigation and examination of evidence.

3. Reporting.

8.1 Planning

The first matter for auditors in planning an audit programme, i.e. the nature, scope and extent of the examination and the evidence required, is to consider the audit objective. Auditors must then plan to carry out such examination and obtain such information and evidence as will enable them to discharge the responsibility that has been undertaken. The audit may be directed towards attesting or expressing an opinion on accounting or other information, or an accounting or other statement, expressing an opinion on an accounting system, or reporting on conduct, performance or achievement (in any of the types of audit that have been discussed). In each case in planning the investigation and examination auditors must decide the degree of confidence they require about the subject matter of the audit and about the content of the audit report or opinion. The test is ultimately a subjective test of what evidence is necessary to take the mind of auditors to a stage when they feel entitled and are entitled to express a professional opinion or make a professional report.

Although the test is essentially subjective, an external objective factor affecting the mind and judgement of an auditor in arriving at a decision on this matter is the evidential requirement which it is understood is necessary to satisfy the professional duty of due care. As has been discussed, not all data or matters can be or will be verified, and auditors need to decide what facts must be ascertained, what information must be obtained, what data and matters must be verified, and how persuasive the relative evidence must be. There are some data or matters the truth of which must be verified and for which compelling or highly persuasive evidence must be obtained or in respect of which there must be compelling evidence that it is highly probable that such evidence could be obtained to enable an auditor to form a judgement in relation to the audit objective. There are some facts which must be established and some information which must be obtained. These are facts and information without which an auditor would not be able to express an opinion or make a report, or could only do so with reservation. These are all issues of materiality. In respect of material matters more persuasive evidence is necessary to produce a higher degree of confidence in the mind of an auditor than is the case of other matters.

The purpose of auditors' obtaining information and examining evidence is to inform themselves about the subject matter of the audit and to carry their mind to a state of confidence about the matters to which they are asked to lend authority or on which they are asked to express an opinion or report. The matter is material if failure to verify it or to obtain information about it affects that state of confidence to an extent which would result in that authority or opinion being qualified or the report being modified. In planning an audit auditors must decide what these matters of materiality are so that evidence of a sufficiently persuasive nature can be sought. The persuasiveness of the evidence may, of course, be derived from the cumulative effect of supporting evidence from a number of different sources pointing to the same conclusion.

In planning the audit of financial statements and data, the issues giving rise to consideration of materiality in auditing can be classified as:

(a) accounting materiality;

(b) key points of control in systems of accounting and control;

(c) critical areas of weakness in systems of accounting and control;

(d) information and data essential for the audit report.

In planning other audits these circumstances may be relevant, but the diversity of circumstances prevents classification of other critical areas. The important principle is that in the direction of any audit auditors must distinguish what is material from what is not in the terms in which it has been defined and plan the audit investigation accordingly, so that in respect of what is material sufficient and sufficiently persuasive evidence is obtained.

Accounting materiality

Materiality in accounting is a matter of materiality in auditing because it identifies the data or information which affect the information content of the financial statement, and which have the potential to affect the understanding and decisions of the persons for whom the data, information or financial statement are prepared. Matters which are material in accounting and financial reporting are material in auditing because an auditor must consider how persuasive the evidence about them must be. Matters of materiality in accounting are among those for which more persuasive evidence is likely to be required, and the audit must be planned accordingly.

Materiality in accounting is a major topic, and it is not possible to deal exhaustively here with all aspects of it. In general terms, a statement, fact, item, data or information is material in accounting if, giving full consideration to the surrounding circumstances as they exist at the time, it is of such a nature that its disclosure (or omission), its mis-statement, or the method of treating it, would be likely to influence the decision or action of the persons for whom the statement, etc. is prepared.

Materiality may be a matter of absolute amount or relative amount (i.e. by reference to or comparison with another amount in the statement, etc.) or it may be qualitative rather than quantitative (the intrinsic nature of the statement, etc. giving it significance for the reader).

Materiality decisions in accounting require a view to be taken of the knowledge and sophistication of the persons for whom the statement or information, etc. is prepared. This matter has already been discussed in Chapter 7. The position taken here is that a sufficient knowledge of accounting to understand the meaning of the statement, etc. and the capability of using that knowledge must be assumed. An action or decision taken on the basis of a financial or accounting statement requires knowledge and capability: except in very few cases, material omissions or mis-statements, or the item of data itself, would not matter to a person who did not have any understanding of the meaning of the statement. Different classes of users can be expected to have different levels of knowledge and capability, and within classes different individuals may have different preferences for what they consider to be the data essential to their rational action or decision; what any individual may consider to be essential is not necessarily constant, but can depend on other attendant circumstances. Writers and official pronouncements, however, have described the user who is to be considered as 'a prudent investor', 'the average prudent investor', 'a reasonable person', 'an informed investor', 'an intelligent reader of the financial statement', and most recently 'those who have a reasonable understanding of business and economic activities and are willing to study the information with reasonable diligence'. It appears an oversimplification to identify one section or sub-group within the principal user group, for example, the prudent informed investor, and to define materiality in relation to that person. If there is information which could properly be disclosed which would affect the decision of the highly sophisticated investment manager, who is a known user, the information is material to that person. In the United Kingdom, the reporting standards for company accounts (and some others) is that they should give a true and fair view. What this requires has not been extensively examined, but it does follow that any information, disclosure, mis-statement, presentation, etc. which would affect the giving and perception of a true and fair view must be material.

Key points of control

The audit investigation and examination of evidence is selective and not exhaustive and comprehensive. Auditors need to exercise judgement in deciding the parts of the investigation which may be restricted to samples and the composition of the samples which are to be brought under scrutiny. For this purpose and for the general purposes of the audit opinion or report, auditors need to form their opinion on the reliability of the system of accounting and control and on the reliability and credibility of the data and information which are included in the financial statement or are used for demonstrating or evaluating performance and accountability. Evaluation of the system involves forming a view as to the key points of control to secure the integrity of the system and of the data and information. The adequacy and efficacy of these key controls are material to auditors as sources of evidence in the verification of the data and information produced by the system. Accordingly, auditors require to have highly persuasive or compelling evidence confirming that these controls do operate. Sufficient and sufficiently persuasive evidence is necessary to take the mind of an auditor to a state of confidence about the reliability of a system and for that confidence to be justified.

Critical areas of weakness

Similarly, evaluating the system of accounting and control involves forming a view on the weaknesses of the system both as it has been designed and how it is operated. Where the weakness affects the confidence of auditors in the reliability of a system as a whole or part of it or the credibility of material data or information, the weakness is a material weakness, and auditors must plan their audit to obtain sufficient and sufficiently persuasive evidence from another source or other sources about the relevant matters to compensate for the system weakness and to produce the required level of confidence in relation to the audit objective.

Information and data essential for the audit report

This includes accounting and non-accounting information and data necessary to an auditor to enable an adequate understanding of the organisation's affairs, the financial statement, the audit objective, and the significance of the audit report.

8.2 Execution: Investigation and Examination of Evidence

The purpose of the audit investigation and examination of evidence is to inform auditors on the matters on which an opinion or report is required; and to find out whether or not data and information presented are what they purport to be and in accordance with the evidence, whether the disclosure and presentation of data and information in statements or otherwise is appropriate and sufficient to meet the defined objective and satisfies any regulatory requirements, and whether in respect of any matter within the scope of the audit there has been dishonesty, irregularity, impropriety or error.

In respect of all of these, auditors require to exercise judgement on whether any departures from the standard of expectation affect their confidence or the terms of their report. Auditors have to decide what discoveries are material to them in the context of the audit objective.

If information which auditors seek is not available, or if any restriction is placed on auditors' investigation or access to evidence, this failure is material to the auditors if it requires reservation or disclaimer in the opinion or report, or makes any report or opinion impossible.

Accounting materiality

In execution of the audit of financial statements and data, as in its planning, there are issues which are material because of their materiality in accounting.

An error, irregularity, mis-statement, misrepresentation, failure to disclose or other departure from expectation, in respect of data, information or statements which is material to users, in the sense that knowledge of it is likely to affect their understanding or decision, is material in auditing. Similarly, the absence of sufficient or sufficiently persuasive evidence for a matter that is material in accounting is also material in auditing. These situations are material in auditing because they affect the terms of an auditor's opinion or report, or an auditor's ability to give an opinion or make a report in discharge of the audit responsibility.

Where the audit examination results in the discovery of material errors or other departures which can be rectified, it would

ormally be expected that this should be done. Even if this is
done, these errors or other departures, and also those which by
eason of their intrinsic nature are not material in accounting,
equire to be considered for their effect on an auditor's confidence
r on the information which is a basis of an auditor's opinion or
eport. In evaluation of the system of accounting and control the
act of an error or other departure having occurred and having
emained undetected until the audit – even if then rectified – is
naterial to auditors if it results in reservations about the reliability
f the system sufficient to occasion reservations about the
redibility of the information produced by the system, and
ccordingly to require the audit examination to be extended to
btain additional evidence from other sources. If this is not
available, the auditor's report or opinion will be affected.

Weaknesses in the system of accounting and control which are
discovered in carrying out the audit need to be evaluated for their
materiality, in the same way as such weaknesses at the planning
tage referred to above.

The audit investigation may produce an issue which is not an
rror or other departure but a difference of opinion between an
auditor and the audited, for example on the treatment of some
tem in valuation, disclosure or presentation. Such an issue has
he same implications for an auditor judged by the criteria of
materiality as an error or departure in relation to the matter in
uestion. An auditor must deal with it according to the effect that
nowledge of it could potentially have on the understanding or
decisions of the user, in the effect of it on the auditor's own
onfidence, or to the relevance of it to the terms of the audit
eport or opinion in discharge of the auditor's terms of reference
nd in fulfilment of the audit purpose.

.3 Reporting

The audit process is completed by the issue of an audit report or
pinion. Communication is important. The terms of the report or
pinion must be calculated to convey to the persons to whom
hey are addressed the information they need and expect to have
according to the terms of reference of the audit. An audit opinion
r report in discharge of the terms of reference and fulfilment of

the audit purpose should give no more information or reassurance than auditors are entitled to give on the basis of the examination that has been made and evidence obtained. At the same time auditors are obliged to carry out such examination and seek such evidence as would entitle them to provide the information or reassurance which the parties want, if it is possible to do so.

Any restriction on auditors' freedom to report or to express an opinion in discharge of the audit terms of reference is material and must be referred to in the report or opinion.

In most audit situations auditors must proceed to an opinion or report on the basis of a sample examination of data and information for which they have the support of systems evidence and substantive evidence. In many cases not all evidence will be compelling or conclusive; evidence is not always available; and the economic limits of time and cost may preclude available evidence from being pursued and produced. In respect of material assertions which are audited, evidence of different types is generally available from different sources. Where the examination discloses errors, irregularities or other departures, or differences of opinion, the materiality of these in relation to the audit objective has to be considered.

Auditors must therefore consider whether the extent and scope of the investigation and the combination of evidence from various sources which has been examined are, taken as a whole, sufficient as a basis of opinion or report, or in what respects these have been inadequate or insufficient. Any inadequacies or insufficiencies have to be considered for their materiality in relation to the auditors' responsibility. If these are material, an audit report, if it can be made, will be conditioned by these circumstances, and an audit opinion must be given with reservations or disclaimed. Matters of materiality for which there has been insufficient or insufficiently persuasive evidence or in respect of which material error or other departure has been found in the course of executing the audit, must also result in comment or reservation in, or disclaimer of opinion.

In the case of financial statements auditors must also consider the possibility of errors, departures from expectations or differences of opinion which have not been disclosed because the examination is only on a sample basis. Such a failure to detect can only matter if knowledge of the error, departure or difference

of opinion, or a combination or aggregation of th
influence the auditor's opinion or report. This is the
the possibility that material errors, etc., that is, ones whic..
influence auditors, remain undetected. There will almost inevitably
be errors, etc. in most parts of the records which have not been
examined. Auditors must therefore form a view as to whether the
possible and probable undisclosed items are material in relation
to the audit objective and the audit responsibility.

As a general rule auditors do not guarantee or certify financial
statements or accounts or offer unqualified assurance that the
records and accounts are free of error and irregularity. The audit
responsibility is such that those to whom the opinion or report is
addressed and who rely on the audit must accept the possibility
that there are remaining errors and irregularities. Auditors must
ensure that in respect of their duty and their responsibility
nothing material remains undisclosed which should have been
detected. The constant dilemma is to reconcile the impossibility
of an auditor's detecting every material error and irregularity and
the users' expectation that the auditor should do so. However, in
respect of that examination which auditors do carry out which is
appropriate in the circumstances, they should be expected to
uncover material items and they must accordingly assess the risk
that they have not done so.

8.4 Criteria

While the concept of audit materiality, the circumstances of its
arising and its implications for auditors can be described in
general terms of principle, it is much more difficult to make this
operational by specifying measurement or other criteria to
distinguish what is material from what is not. It is not possible
within the limits of this text to do more than indicate some of the
issues.

The relationship between materiality and the quality of evidence
is clearly related to the systematic relationship between evidence
and auditor confidence, which is an unexplored area. There are
no systematic measurements for the reliability of the system of
accounting and control. Auditors must identify the key points of
control and the weaknesses of the system in order to decide the

persuasive quality of evidence required, of which they are the sole judges. Statistical analysis may focus the issues for judgement but does not eliminate the use of judgement.

Accounting materiality and the materiality of errors, irregularities, mis-statements and other departures may be qualitative or quantitative in their significance. Some qualitative issues may be identified and classified in advance, but they are most likely to be specific to the particular audit. Guidelines can be no more than indications of the kind of circumstances which are likely to be relevant. A regulatory, legal or other requirement relating to data or information makes these items material in audit planning and execution requiring highly persuasive evidence, and makes error, mis-statement, misrepresentation, a failure to make a required disclosure, or any other departure from the requirement in relation to these items material in reporting. The nature of an error, mis-statement, misrepresentation or other failure may have a significance for its implications irrespective of the amount involved and make the item material for its effect on the audit investigation, its effect on auditor confidence, and its relevance to the audit report. The status or appointment of a person involved in fraud or other irregularity may similarly have a significance for its implications and make the item material for reporting irrespective of the amount involved.

The quantitative characteristic of accounting items and errors and other irregularities can probably be described by common criteria. It is generally represented that quantitative items are material by reason of their absolute or relative significance. What is absolute significance in one case may not be so in another, so that both of these require some base line of significance. The most common proposal is that effect on profit (net profit, gross profit, average profit, anticipated profit, or other variation on profit) provides an adequate measure of materiality; although this is an oversimplification, there will be circumstances when it will be acceptable. There is no single correct base against which items can be universally measured to determine their materiality. A table of amounts, relative amounts and ratios could be established as guidelines for industries or types of organisation, but this might be found to be more dangerous than helpful when the other specific variables, for example economic conditions, loan conditions, the highly specialised nature of inventories, the olatility of profit, and so on, are considered. It does appear to be more appropriate that for each business or organisation the auditor should establish a table of specific amounts, relative amounts and ratios to be used as guidelines in that case. The border zone approach may be a useful one, stipulating the points below which the item may be considered immaterial, above which the item will be regarded as material unless there is a strong argument against, and between which the auditor would require to give individual consideration and to exercise professional judgement.

After all factors are taken into account, materiality in auditing remains very much a matter of judgement. Qualitative indicators and quantitative criteria will be useful as aids to judgement, but in the present state of knowledge and understanding of the use of audit evidence reliance must be placed on the knowledge, skill and experience of auditors and on their appreciation of the importance of the issue.

Standards IV

IV

Standards

Introduction to Part IV

Auditing is important to society. The audit of industrial and commercial concerns, public boards, state corporations, public utilities, local and central government departments, and private associations for business, charitable, recreational or other purposes is a matter of both public and private concern, with important social implications. This is particularly so in the larger units, whether in the public or private sector or in government or administration, where audit is a critical part of the machinery for securing accountability and control. The audit requirement in different organisations is a product of and is dependent on the culture, the social and political philosophy and the values of the society in which the organisations operate. The audit therefore requires to change to meet the changing expectations of a changing society.

The relative importance, in various organisations, in different societies and at different times, of honesty, regularity, efficiency, effectiveness, social responsibility, and so on, as criteria of accountability and, accordingly, of audit significance has changed and will no doubt continue to do so. The machinery of accountability and the framework within which the audit takes place are also dependent on the nature of the society, and so will change. These are changes which can be seen to be taking place. Some of the changes require statutory or regulatory authority, but some are the product of an evolutionary interpretation of the audit concept.

It is not surprising, therefore, that there is considerable public interest in auditing, and there are increasing signs of dissatisfaction both in the public and private sectors with the adequacy of present audit arrangements, the terms of reference of auditors, and the scope of audit reports. Critical comment may sometimes fail to distinguish the shortcomings of the system from deficiencies in performance; and criticism may be ill-founded due to lack of understanding of the limitations of audit examination or to unrealistic expectations of what can be achieved within the economic constraints of time and cost and the technical constraints of practicability. However, because audit must be responsive to the changing needs of society, and standards of professional performance must aspire to the level of public expectations, it is necessary to pay attention to the criticisms that are made.

This is the context and environment in which the professional performance of the auditor has to be considered. The organisations which are subject to audit are changing, the nature of accountability is changing, the organisation and processing of information are changing and becoming more complex, and a better educated, more informed, more challenging, more demanding, more articulate and better organised public, or sets of interest groups, have expectations in relation to what audit can achieve, and these are becoming uncompromisingly more specific.

The growing public interest in auditing is not surprising; what is perhaps surprising is the lack of intellectual curiosity about the subject which has been shown both by practising auditors and by academic scholars, and the little attention that has been given to the philosophical, sociological or organisation theory foundations of auditing. Auditing is such an important part of the social framework, as part of the machinery of social control to secure the accountability of individuals and organisations and in establishing the credibility of information which is used for important economic decisions, that it is remarkable that the process by which these results are achieved has not been the subject of rigorous research and analysis. The technical and ethical standards by reference to which auditors work are matters of great social significance.

Auditing is an activity which requires education, training and experience and which, in its execution, requires knowledge, skill and the exercise of judgement. The primary objective and outcome of an audit is the expression of a professional opinion by an auditor which can be relied on as a basis of action by those to whom it is addressed. Auditing is a professional activity, and auditors are personally liable, as a result of any negligent failure on their part in carrying out their professional work, for loss or damage suffered by a person to whom they owe a duty. Whether there has been a failure will depend on whether the performance is satisfactory when tested against a standard.

Auditors' standards, however, are important not only as a basis of establishing responsibility at law. The perceived standards are vital to establishing the confidence of those who use audit opinions and reports that these are reliable and authoritative in relation to the matters to which they refer. Public confidence in the audit and as a consequence its social value is only sustained by a belief that auditors' standards of competence, objectivity, independence and professionalism are satisfactory. It is important, therefore, that the principles by which these standards are determined should be understood. It is necessary, too, that operational standards or guidelines to give effect to these principles should be established, that arrangements should be made to ensure that these standards are observed and maintained, and that appropriate action should be taken if there are failures to comply with the standards.

It is the issues of due care, professional standards and quality control which will now be considered.

Due Care and Negligence

9

A professional opinion is the product of an individual's judgement based on the requisite knowledge, training, experience and skill which give the person the right to have that opinion respected. It must, however, be an opinion which is arrived at with due care after deliberation and the exercise of the special skill and expertise which are professed. Otherwise, the opinion would be worth no more than that of a person with no special qualification and skill in the subject, and whoever relied on it would be misled as to its authority. It follows, therefore, that a person claiming to express a professional opinion must be expected to have taken due care, that is to say a minimum adequate degree of diligence and care in enquiry and consideration to discharge their professional responsibility. A failure to do so is likely to be construed in law as negligence in the same way as other failures to take due care with consequences for other parties affected by the failure.

In the United Kingdom – and similarly in many other countries – the general principle of law with regard to the standard of performance of a professional man or woman is that those who carry out work which demands a particular skill must not only exercise reasonable care, but they must measure up to the standard of competence of the ordinary practitioner claiming that skill. They are required to exercise that degree of proficiency and care which is expected to be exercised by the ordinary skilful, diligent and careful practitioner engaged in similar practice under the same or similar circumstances.

The principles for auditors were enunciated in the United Kingdom in legal cases in 1895 and 1896 in the following terms:

An auditor is not bound to do more than exercise reasonable care and skill in making enquiries and investigations . . . he must not certify what he does not believe to be true, and he must take reasonable care and skill before he believes what he certifies is true. What is reasonable care in any particular case must depend upon the circumstances of that case. (*London and General Bank (No. 2)*, (1895) 2 Ch. 673)

It is the duty of an auditor to bring to bear on the work he has to perform, that skill, care and caution which a reasonably competent, careful and cautious auditor would use. What is reasonable skill, care and caution must depend on the particular circumstances of each case. (*Kingston Cotton Mill Co. (No. 2)*, (1896) 2 Ch. 279)

As the measure of the standard required of an auditor, this was affirmed in 1967:

I am not clear that the quality of the auditor's duty has changed in any relevant respect since 1896. Basically that duty has always been to audit the company's accounts with reasonable care and skill. The real ground on which Re Kingston Cotton Mill Co. (No. 2) is I think capable of being distinguished is that the standards of reasonable care and skill are, on the expert evidence, more exacting today than those which prevailed in 1896. (*Thomas Gerrard & Son Ltd.*, (1967) 2 All ER 525)

A similar view was taken in the Supreme Court of New South Wales in 1970:

It is beyond question that when an auditor, professing as he does to possess the requisite professional skills, enters into a contract to perform certain tasks as auditor, he promises to perform such tasks using that degree of skill and care as is reasonable in the circumstances as they then exist. That is the limit of his promise. That is the bare statement of the legal obligation and in the end the court must come back in any case

to the legal proposition and apply it to the court's views on the facts found.

And:

> The legal duty, namely, to audit the accounts with reasonable skill and care, remains the same, but reasonableness and skill in auditing must bring to account and be directed towards the changed circumstances referred to. Reasonable skill and care calls for changed standards to meet changed conditions or changed understanding of dangers and in this sense standards are more exacting today than in 1896. This the audit profession has rightly accepted, and by change in emphasis in their procedures and in some changed procedures have acknowledged that due skill and care calls for some different approaches.

The opinion, however, goes on to make an important point:

> It is not a question of the court requiring higher standards because the profession has adopted higher standards. It is a question of the court applying the law which by its content expects such reasonable standards as will meet the circumstances of today, including modern conditions of business and knowledge concerning them.

However, it confirms the importance of expert evidence:

> now as formerly, standards and practices adopted by the profession to meet current circumstances provide a sound guide to the court in determining what is reasonable. (*Pacific Acceptance Corporation Ltd.* v. *Forsyth and Ors.*, Supreme Court of New South Wales in Commercial Causes, 8 January 1970)

This general interpretation of the position is also confirmed by Dickerson (1966):

> Since, in actions against professional men, the law will normally adopt the standards of the profession, it follows that an allegation of negligence will be dismissed if the defendant shows that he

conformed to the practices accepted as proper by a responsible section of the profession, even though others in the profession take a different view. (Dickerson, 1966, p. 2)

Interpretation of this last quotation without reservation may be too reassuring a view of the position. While the court will have regard to expert evidence, it is inherent in the position that a court of law would require to test and be satisfied as to the adequacy of the standards of care and skill as established by that evidence. Auditors have had salutary reminders in recent years that while expert evidence as to prevailing practice may be very persuasive, it is not conclusive as to the standard the law requires, and is not binding on a court of law. The fact that proof of compliance with generally accepted standards is evidence which may be very persuasive but not necessarily conclusive, was made explicit in the direction to the jury in the Continental Vending case (*USA* v. *Simon and Ors.*, United States Court of Appeals, 1969), and was stated very clearly in the Pacific Acceptance case:

The propriety of taking or not taking a particular audit step depends on the circumstances met in the particular audit . . . in the end the court must make its own decision on the particular circumstances of the case, using the procedures adopted by others as but a general guide as to how others attack a particular but somewhat similar problem . . . When the conduct of an auditor is in question in legal proceedings it is not the province of the audit profession itself to determine what is the legal duty of auditors or to determine what reasonable skill and care require to be done in a particular case, although what others do or what is usually done is relevant to the question of whether there had been a breach of duty. It follows, if the audit profession or most of them fail to adopt some step which despite their practice was reasonably required of them, such failure does not cease to be a breach of duty because all or most of them did the same. (*Pacific Acceptance Corporation Ltd.* v. *Forsyth and Ors.*)

These extracts of opinions are taken from different jurisdictions. They are not set out as a complete and comprehensive statement of the law in any of these. They have been chosen to illustrate the concept of due care in terms of the principle involved rather than as precedents which would necessarily precisely apply in any one country. It is believed that they fairly represent in general terms the standard which auditors require to observe.

The ultimate authority rests with a court of law, and the difficult question is to contemplate in what circumstances the court would reject the standard as testified by expert witnesses, on the grounds that it fell below what 'was reasonably required of them' (Pacific Acceptance). This is no doubt an uncomfortable position for auditors, and it has perhaps been too readily assumed by many in the past that to conform to prevailing practice – however difficult it may have been for the practising auditor to find out what that was – was the criterion to apply. Auditors are understandably concerned at the possibility that courts might endorse the unreasonable and impracticable expectations of the public or a particular section of it in specific circumstances.

It is therefore a matter of the greatest importance and urgency for the auditing profession constantly to review and revise its practice in accordance with the expansion of knowledge, the development of improved techniques and the enhancement of practical capability. The profession must also be sensitive and responsive to societal expectations while at the same time realistically recognising the practical and economic constraints which prevent the satisfying of some of the reassurances which an anxious and troubled society would like to have.

There is an onus on the profession, in justification of the social and economic privileges, status and benefits which its members enjoy, to go as far as possible to meet the societal expectations and to be able to demonstrate that it has done so. If the profession has been rigorous, thorough and systematic in what it does in this respect, this must be the strongest possible basis on which to persuade the courts that the standards adopted by the profession should be accepted, and that any other public expectation should be refuted as impossible of fulfilment. However, change and development in all relevant spheres are continuous and in some cases substantial, so that the burden on the practitioner to maintain the 'peculiar skill' which 'he holds himself out to the public as possessing' is a considerable one.

Explaining their concept of the prudent practitioner, Mautz

and Sharaf (1961) support the proposition of the need for auditors continually to raise the level of their performance:

> **The prudent practitioner will keep abreast of developments in his area of competence; he will seek knowledge of methods of perpetrating, concealing and detecting irregularities . . . he must take such steps as are necessary to familiarise himself with developments in auditing. No reasonable man would expect to maintain his competence in a dynamic and growing profession without continuing study and effort.** (Mautz and Sharaf, 1961, p. 138)

Elaborating this general proposition to take account of the legal precepts which have been enunciated, namely that

(a) the requirements of due care must depend on the circumstances of the case,

(b) the standards of reasonable care and skill can be expected to be more exacting than hitherto,

(c) changed standards are called for to meet changed conditions or changed understanding of dangers,

(d) these standards must be adequate for current circumstances including modern conditions of business and knowledge concerning them,

demonstrates dramatically the extent to which developments of recent years require auditors to expand their competence and raise the level of their performance.

The size and complexity of organisations which are subject to audit, the complexity and implications of the transactions in which they are engaged, the sophistication of records, decision-making techniques, information systems, management and administration, the expansion of knowledge and growth in the understanding of business management, administration and government, the range and scope of issues of business policy and public policy, the evolution of more comprehensive and more demanding criteria of accountability, and other related factors together demand of auditors an increasingly high intellectual quality and a maturity of understanding to provide the capacity to make the judgements which discharge of their responsibilities to the community requires.

Summarising the position, an auditor is engaged in a profession and must exercise independent judgement in forming an opinion. An auditor must possess the degree of skill commonly possessed by others in the same employment, which must be adequate and relevant to the requirements of current circumstances, and exercised with reasonable care and diligence. While adequacy, relevance and reasonableness will have regard to what other practitioners do, the overriding test is whether the practices of auditors satisfy a standard of what may reasonably be required of them. What may reasonably be required of auditors in terms of the adequacy, relevance and reasonableness of their practices will have regard to societal expectations and to changes in knowledge and the conditions in which the audited organisations operate.

Standards of Practice

10

While auditors have a legal duty to act with the skill, diligence and care which may reasonably be required, having regard to societal expectations and the relevant circumstances, the law has not attempted to define in detailed terms the degree of skill which they must possess or the diligence and care which are expected; nor has the law specified what auditors must do to advise themselves as a basis of giving an opinion. These matters have been left to the individual auditor to decide in a particular case, and to the auditing profession collectively, where appropriate, to make recommendations on what would be generally applicable.

10.1 Standard of the Ordinary Practitioner

Auditors must recognise and accept that it is on their own knowledge, experience, skill and judgement that they must depend in deciding the enquiries and investigations to be made and the nature and extent of evidence to be obtained to enable them to form an opinion. Auditors have a professional duty to interpret their responsibility and the kind of performance which the user public can reasonably expect, and to charge themselves to work by reference to these criteria. If they fail to do so they do not discharge their duty. It is, however, a matter of the greatest importance to auditors to know what is the practice of the 'ordinary skilful, diligent and careful practitioner engaged in similar practice', which is a yard-stick, perhaps the principal yard-stick, by which they may be judged. If auditors depart from or fall short of what is commonly done, they do so at their peril; and if they do so knowingly, they are on notice that they may have to justify their variation from the norm. By exercise of their own judgement auditors may in some or all circumstances work to more exacting standards; or they may conscientiously disagree with the appropriateness of practices which are commonly followed and adopt different practices. It is essential, however, that they should know what practices are commonly followed.

10.2   A Conceptual Standard

While these are matters of professional judgement for auditors for which they are expected to have special professional competence, they do need to have some theoretical or philosophical principles on which to base practice. Reference has already been made (see Chapter 6) to Limperg's 'Theory of Inspired Confidence' of which the normative core is that 'the accountant is obliged to carry out his work in such a way that he does not betray the expectations which he evokes in the sensible layman; and, conversely, the accountant may not arouse greater expectations than can be justified by the work done'. Limperg was concerned with the social dimension of the audit and the responsibility of the auditor to the community at large. He saw the general function of the auditor in society as being derived from the need for expert and independent opinion based on that examination:

> The function is rooted in the confidence that society places in the effectiveness of the audit and in the opinion of the accountant. This confidence is therefore a condition for the existence of that function; if the confidence is betrayed, the function, too, is destroyed, since it becomes useless . . . he must perform the work necessary to justify the confidence in his audit and in his opinion. If that work does not meet this requirement – particularly if the work is done in such a way, to such a limited extent that confidence is betrayed in the end – then the function

too loses its purport; it misses a real basis and has no *raison d'être.* (Limperg, 1985, pp. 16 and 17)

This brief statement of the Limperg thesis expresses eminently the conceptual basis for the auditor's approach to the standard of performance required. It recognises that that standard should be based on a proper perception of the societal expectation for reassurance, an appreciation of the confidence which is placed in the audit opinion, and an understanding of the kind of enquiry and examination which is necessary to justify that confidence and satisfy that expectation. The questions for auditors are how to translate this into operational terms and how to advise themselves of the views of other auditors on the practices to be adopted.

10.3 Responsibility of the Auditing Profession

It has already been stated in Part II of this book that as a basis of public confidence auditors require to be qualified and to have acquired the relevant professional skill by education, training and experience. In the process of 'qualifying' in an approved manner auditors should have learned by training, instruction and experience the current professional practices and standards of the 'ordinary skilful, diligent and careful practitioner'. However, the process of qualifying cannot expect to encompass all audit situations during the training period and it cannot, of course, deal with the continuing advance of knowledge and the social evolution of audit expectation subsequent to the date of qualification. While auditors as members of a profession must accept a personal responsibility to keep themselves updated, the auditing profession institutionally has both a social duty and an understandable interest, particularly within the framework of self-regulation, to have a concern for standards of competence of both entrants to and members of the auditing profession, and with the success of the profession in satisfying the social need and discharging its obligations in the public interest.

It is not surprising, therefore, that the auditing profession has seen the merit of collective action in the dissemination of information based on a mixture of research, study and distillation of experience on matters of auditing practice. The auditing profession and its representative organisations may also perceive some benefit in authoritative public statements in the field of audit practice for the information of interested user groups and more particularly for the guidance of courts and other tribunals which have occasion to consider the adequacy of audit performance. The pronouncements on auditing – Statements, Standards, Recommendations, Guidelines – issued by the international, regional and national professional accountancy bodies, for example the International Federation of Accountants, the Union Européenne des Experts Comptables Economiques et Financiers,[1] and the Institutes and the Association in the United Kingdom and Ireland are indicative of this professional concern. Statements issued by The Audit Commission for Local Authorities in England and Wales and by the Commission for Local Authority Accounts in Scotland for the guidance of auditors are further evidence of a concern to establish standards of practice.[2]

10.4 Professional Standards, Guidelines and Statements

The extension of activity in this field raises difficult questions of the status of the above-mentioned authoritative pronouncements which require a careful analysis of the purpose and extent of the guidance that is embraced in them. The International Federation of Accountants (IFAC), in the Explanatory Foreword to the International Auditing Guidelines, states that the objective in this regard is to develop and issue guidelines on generally accepted auditing practices and on the form and content of audit reports with the intention of improving the degree of uniformity of auditing practices throughout the world. It is acknowledged that within each country local regulations, which may be either of a statutory nature or in the form of statements issued by the regulatory or professional bodies in the countries concerned, or both, govern to a greater or lesser degree the practices followed in the auditing of financial information. It is stated that, while the statements on auditing already published in many countries differ in form and content, cognisance is taken of such statements and differences, and in the light of such knowledge the International Auditing Guidelines are intended for international acceptance. As to the status of the International Auditing Guidelines, the

IFAC states that they do not override the local regulations governing the audit of financial information in a particular country. In accordance with the constitution of the IFAC, member bodies subscribe to the objective and agree to work towards implementation of the Guidelines when and to the extent practicable under local circumstances.

The member organisations of the Union Européenne des Experts Comptables Economiques et Financiers (UEC) undertake to support UEC auditing statements by either bringing to the notice of their members the content of UEC definitive statements or alternatively incorporating in their national auditing standards the principles on which UEC definitive statements are based; using their best endeavours, in those countries where audit procedures are prescribed by law, to get the laws adapted accordingly; and using their best endeavours to ensure that bodies responsible for the maintenance of professional standards are aware of UEC auditing statements.

The Councils of the professional accountancy bodies in the United Kingdom[3] distinguish between Auditing Standards, which prescribe the basic principles and practices which members who assume responsibility as auditors are expected to follow, and Auditing Guidelines, which give guidance on procedures by which the Auditing Standards may be applied. With respect to the Auditing Standards, auditors are informed that they are expected to observe them and that apparent failures to observe them may be enquired into and disciplinary action may result. 'In the observance of Auditing Standards', it is stated, 'the auditor must exercise his judgement in determining both the auditing procedures necessary in the circumstances to afford a reasonable basis for his opinion and the wording of his report'. The Auditing Standard on the Audit Report requires the auditor to refer expressly in his report to 'whether the financial statements have been audited in accordance with approved Auditing Standards'.

There are a number of arguments in favour of the promulgation of Auditing Standards and Guidelines to which reference has already been made: the dissemination of information to auditors on matters of practice, for the information of user groups, and for the guidance of courts, to which may be added for the instruction of students and trainees. Auditing Standards and Guidelines approved by representative professional bodies should conform to current general practice (but see the further comment on p. 158) and should, accordingly, be valuable to auditors who need to be aware of the practices commonly adopted by others in the same or similar circumstances. Similarly, while not specific to any given set of circumstances such as would be required in a legal action, they should be useful as a general guide in the courts to provide a background for the specific evidence which will be advanced in a particular case. What must be examined, however, is the authoritative status of the Standards and Guidelines and the consequential effect on the position, responsibility and liability of auditors.

10.5   Authority of Professional Standards, Guidelines and Statements

It would appear that Auditing Standards which prescribe basic principles will be persuasive, although not conclusive, evidence of the standard of the ordinary skilful, diligent and careful practitioner. As for the other pronouncements on auditing, although they are not given quite the same status by the professional bodies, it seems probable that their persuasive value will not be very much less as regards the standard expected of the practitioner in the situations to which they refer. Auditors are required, professionally, to follow the Standards. Other pronouncements are not definitive, and auditors are expected to continue to exercise their judgement in determining procedures. Auditors, however, in the discharge of their professional duty, must exercise their judgement in respect of the whole audit responsibility. In considering the persuasiveness of the Standards and Guidance Statements as authoritative evidence of the required standard, it is possible that a court of law or other tribunal would not distinguish between the two. Indeed, if it is an auditor's procedures that are in question, the content of the Guidance Statements may be of more significance and more telling as a measure of adequacy of an auditor's performance.

It is not, however, within the competence of any professional body to override an auditor's judgement or deny an auditor's duty to exercise it. The strong persuasive force which the professional bodies give to Auditing Standards must, therefore, be something short of prescriptive. In the exercise of their own judgement auditors may wisely decide to follow the Auditing Standards. If these Standards are well conceived it is likely that they most generally will do so. In the exercise of individual judgement an auditor may, however, decide to depart from them. If an auditor's performance comes under review the matter for consideration is not whether there was a departure from the Auditing Standards and Guidelines but whether what was done or failed to be done was negligent, or was evidence of inefficiency or incompetence amounting to professional misconduct.

In promulgating statements of auditing standards and of guidance the professional bodies are seeking to maintain and to raise the standard of auditing practice by informing auditors of the standards of performance by reference to which their practice should be guided. These standards have an immediate authority by virtue of their source and the fact that they have secured the approval of the ruling bodies of the profession. That authority will be sustained only if the standards are found to be well conceived, and is subordinate to the ultimate authority of the court in a case which goes to law. Their authority will, in the final analysis, be derived from their relevance and appropriateness in social terms, and it is for this that the professional bodies must strive.

The legal authorities quoted make clear that standards as evidenced by expert witnesses will be highly persuasive but not conclusive and that a failure to adopt some practice which the court is persuaded might reasonably be required is nonetheless a breach of duty, even if all the profession would have done the same. This means that auditors are always on notice to exercise their own judgement as to the applicability of a Standard or Guidance Statement promulgated by the professional body. It is necessary to distinguish between an auditor disregarding or being ignorant of a Standard and an auditor setting a Standard aside as inappropriate. The vital test for auditors is whether they are confident that their performance will satisfy the standard of the law. Conforming to the approved Standards is a means to an end and not an end in itself.

It is important, therefore, that the auditing standard-making process should be dynamic, progressive and open. Auditing Standards which are no more than a codification of practice based on past experience are, except in the most basic principles of the audit role, likely to be constantly out of date. Past experience is an important and essential contribution, but it is not sufficient on its own. The auditing standard-making process requires to have a basis of multidisciplinary research to ensure that auditors receive the best guidance as to what standard of performance is necessary to satisfy the societal need and expectation.

Quality Control

11

Auditors have both a legal duty and a professional obligation to work to the highest standard which can reasonably be expected to discharge the responsibility that is placed on them. Auditors must carry out such an investigation in nature and extent, and have sufficient evidence to take their mind to a state of confidence about the matter on which an opinion has to be expressed or a report given. The level of confidence must be related to the expectations of the persons to whom the opinion or report is addressed and be precisely expressed in that report or opinion. That is the individual, personal responsibility of the auditor. In the discharge of that responsibility an auditor must decide the detail of the investigation that is to be carried out – what is to be investigated and what is the objective of the investigation – the kind of evidence that will be sought and the procedures and practices that will be followed.

It is not enough, however, for auditors to specify the procedures: these procedures and practices must then be followed and executed competently, although there must be scope within the procedures for the exercise of initiative based on judgement as a result of the discoveries of the investigation. In addition, in planning and executing an audit auditors must have regard to and generally adhere to the auditing standards and guidelines issued by the professional bodies and to the operational implications of decisions of the courts.

All this would be difficult enough if auditors were responsible

159

only for their own work. The nature of auditing, however, is such that only occasionally and only in the smallest audits do principal auditors themselves carry out all the work of the audit. Apart from these, all audits involve a number of persons of different capabilities. In the largest audits, for example, of international groups of companies, a very large number of persons is engaged. This means that for the principal auditors who have ultimately to take personal responsibility for the audit opinion or report, whether in their own name or in the name of a firm, arrangements for the delegation of responsibility for audit work must be made, which involves direction, supervision and control.

The scale of audits and the complexity of auditing which have resulted from developments in the twentieth century, and the consequential serious consequences of audit failure, make it imperative that there is a thoroughly systematic and comprehensive formalised approach to direction, supervision and control in carrying out an audit. Arrangements for what is now correctly described as 'quality control' are an important aspect of audit management: it is important, therefore, that the underlying principles should be established.

The auditing profession institutionally and the professional bodies have an interest in the maintenance of standards of practice and, in the discharge of their responsibility in the public interest, they have a duty to be concerned if auditors individually or collectively fall below the standard which the public is reasonably entitled to expect. Because of the public interest factor the state also has a concern and responsibility. This may be exercised directly, through the appointed professional bodies, or through the state's regulatory agency. The professional bodies, therefore, acting for the profession in a self-regulating environment, or the appointed agency where auditors are regulated under the direct supervision of the state, require to have a procedure for monitoring the operational standards of auditors. Circumstances will determine whether the monitoring authority should be actively involved or whether it should be reactive only in the event of failures being brought to its attention: this will be discussed more fully below.

11.1 Public Confidence

In a profession whose authority is dependent among other things on public confidence and whose social function requires a commitment to the public interest, a demonstrable concern, individually and collectively on the part of the members of the profession, to control and maintain the highest quality in its work, is a matter of basic principle. The basis of continuing public confidence and trust in professional competence is a belief that the standards of the members of the profession will be maintained and can be relied on. Professional designation of individuals signifies to the public that their standards are satisfactory and there is therefore an obligation on the profession collectively and on the individual personally to ensure that they are. It is essential, therefore, that auditors, individually and collectively, should take appropriate action to reassure the public and those who use audit reports and opinions that these reports and opinions, as a result of the basis on which they are arrived at, are competently prepared, reliable and give credibility to the matters to which they refer. It is necessary in current circumstances to take more positive action than hitherto to demonstrate to the public that the auditing profession, individually and collectively, acts in a way which controls and maintains the quality of its performance.

Auditors' accountability

Following increasing concern about the public accountability of large corporations and a new realisation that a crucial element in the machinery of social control and in monitoring accountability is the audit, the question is being raised as to whether the profession which is responsible for auditing these large corporations is itself sufficiently publicly accountable. This is a relatively new issue and not all the implications have been explored. It is, however, one of the factors contributing to the increased public interest in auditing standards, and it emphasises further the burden on the auditing profession to re-examine the organisation and procedures by which a satisfactory standard of performance is maintained.

Professional standards of the audit firm

Maintaining auditing standards is not only a matter of defining standards of practice and procedure; it requires also the introduction and operation of the organisational arrangements necessary to ensure that the practices and procedures are implemented and that standards are in fact maintained. Although the concept of quality control in auditing is not new, it has become more comprehensive and more significant as the means of manifesting externally the discharge of professional responsibility. What is at issue now is not only the professional standards of the individual but the professional standards of the audit firm as an organisational entity. Quality control is now concerned with the policies and procedures which are designed to establish, monitor, review and secure adherence to professional standards in all aspects of the organisation of the professional practice.

Responsibility of the professional bodies

The primary responsibility for action on quality control measures rests with auditors and audit firms, and in the interest of public confidence the existence and operation of quality control policies and procedures must be a matter of public knowledge. The professional bodies, which have an institutional responsibility for the standards and competence of their members and the public status and reputation of their profession, also have a responsibility; as a minimum they must be satisfied that adequate quality control policies and procedures are in operation. This does not mean that the professional bodies can meet their obligation by monitoring adherence to the requirements of published auditing standards in individual audit engagements and seeking the means of enforcing them. The issue is a more general and fundamental one. The professional bodies need to take such measures as are necessary to have reasonable confidence that auditors and audit firms are operating policies and procedures to achieve a high standard of auditing and public accountability, of which complying with published auditing standards is only a part.

There are different ways in which the professional bodies could discharge their responsibilities. The question at issue is whether it is sufficient for the professional bodies to be satisfied that acceptable policies and procedures are promulgated and that audit firms are committed to them, or whether the situation calls for some system of inspection.

It is important to appreciate, however, that no system of auditing standards, recommendations and guidelines, review or inspection will eliminate the possibility of human failure or guarantee to the public that mistakes will not be made. Auditors have an individual responsibility, and there are remedies available against them if they fail to meet their responsibilities. Although the views of the professional bodies on standards, policies and procedures, if well conceived, will carry great authority, the individual auditor has a personal responsibility in each set of circumstances to be satisfied as to their adequacy and appropriateness. Auditors must remember that, in the case of dispute, the final judgement as to their adequacy lies not with the professional bodies but with the courts.

The auditing profession is not alone in having to meet a more explicit public concern about its standards and how it conducts its affairs. The principles of professional responsibility and integrity are no longer taken on trust by a sceptical public. The professions have constantly to justify themselves to society to be allowed to continue to enjoy the perceived – however illusory – social and economic benefits of status and privilege. The paradox is that, although the professions are attacked for what they are, the same censorious public continues to expect to be able to rely on them for the values and services which they represent. Auditors must, therefore, come to terms with this new situation. Auditing is a vital and expanding part of the machinery of social control and its standards are important for the standards of society. Auditing standards, policies and procedures for quality control must therefore be conceived positively and dynamically in the context of the evolving needs and expectations of society and be seen to be not only well conceived but effectively implemented.

11.2 Quality Control Policies and Procedures

The nature and importance of auditing standards have been dealt with already in Chapters 9 and 10. The general principle governing the quality control policies and procedures is that they should include all matters which are relevant to maintaining and enhancing the standards necessary to meet auditors' professional obligations. The matters which have to be dealt with can be conveniently grouped under four main heads:

1. General policy: principles of practice; independence; clients.

2. Personnel: engagement; training; professional development; assignment.

3. Audit management and practice: training; assignment; direction; supervision; consultation.

4. Inspection and review: internal; post audit; inter-office; practice inspection.

General policy

The attitude and philosophy of the individual auditor and/or the firm in relation to the execution of professional assignments and the standards to be applied and achieved must be sufficiently explicit to be understood by everyone in the audit firm and must permeate all its activities. While quality control will be exercised through systematic instruction, direction, supervision and review, which will be the subject of comprehensive documentation, it is not possible to cover every facet and contingency. An essential element of the total process is the creation of an atmosphere or ethos of quality standards in the audit firm. This is less tangible than documentation, but will be reflected in the documentation as well as in the attitudes and performance of the people in the firm. It will also be reflected in the detailed rules and guidelines of the audit firm which should be prepared, for example, to interpret the operational application of the principles of audit independence, to explain how audit difficulties should be dealt with, to define the conditions under which new clients will be accepted, and to indicate circumstances in which termination of an appointment should be considered.

These are matters which in a comprehensive system of quality control should be the subject of specific written guidance setting out the criteria which will generally apply and from which departure may be made only after due consideration and consultation.

Personnel

The standard of professional work is dependent on the performance of individuals; arguably the most important elements in quality control are the personal standards and the standards of competence, diligence and execution of work by personnel at all levels in the audit firm.

Quality control starts with the care taken and the criteria applied in the selection and engagement of staff with the attributes of character and personality as well as the capability for the appointments for which they are engaged. This has to be associated with a personnel policy embracing training, continuing professional education, career counselling and development, and planned personal advancement to maintain professional competence and to secure a balanced staff structure.

Associated with these measures to create professional capability are the arrangements to select for assignments staff with the requisite knowledge, training, experience and the appropriate personal qualities for the special features of each set of circumstances. It is, of course, a professional obligation on the part of the individual auditor not to accept appointment to an audit for which they do not have the requisite capability (see Chapter 5).

Audit management and practice

Having selected the appropriate staff, quality control requires that they should be properly instructed in relation to the particular audit, both generally and with regard to any special features, that they should receive any additional training which the assignment requires, and that their work should then be subject to supervision and review to ensure that the firm's practices are being observed and standards adhered to. This requires a properly structured staff on each assignment, with an allocation of tasks and specific responsibilities; audit programmes supported by audit manuals and technical instructions; on-the-job supervision with scope for consultation and reference back on technical issues and problems arising; the inspection of working papers and programme completion; and the review of action and disposal on issues arising before completion of the audit.

Inspection and review

The final stages in quality control are the inspection and review before signing the audit opinion or report, and the post-audit reviews.

The audit principal responsible for signing the opinion or report will, of course, carry out an inspection and review of the working papers, the completed programme and the issues arising, with such personal discussion with the staff involved as is considered necessary, in addition to personal involvement in the audit and resolution of the audit issues arising as may be necessary in each case. At the final stage before signing, particularly in larger audits, another audit principal from the same office of the audit firm who has not so far been involved in the audit may review the working papers and programme and disposal of the issues arising to bring to bear a second opinion on these matters and on consideration of whether the firm's standards, practices and procedures have been adhered to.

Following the issue of the report or opinion quality control requires the operation of a system of post-audit review. This may be a comprehensive review, by specially assigned technical staff of the office, or of the firm as a whole if there is more than one office, of the working papers, the completed programme and the record of audit issues arising. The objective is not only to make a systematic and considered appraisal of whether standards are being maintained and practices adhered to, but also to find out if there are any general practice issues of wider relevance and interest and any areas in which change and/or improvement in standards or practices should be considered. As part of the post-audit review there may be an inter-office review in which a test selection of the audit papers of one office are reviewed by a principal from another office of the same firm. The purpose of this is to establish on a co-operative basis where mutual interests are at stake, whether there is scope for change or improvement in the management of the firm's audits.

11.3 Practice Inspection

All these measures for quality control are taken within the firm. Auditors and audit firms have the primary responsibility. The professional bodies have a responsibility to be satisfied that policies and procedures for quality control have been adopted and that professional standards are being maintained. The state has a concern to protect the public interest. There has to be considered, therefore, whether the effective organisation of quality control requires any procedures for review and inspection external to and independent of the audit firm and, if so, how this should be arranged.

There are two principal objectives in developing more systematic measures of quality control: firstly, to meet the auditors' professional obligations of providing services to the highest possible standard in relation to users' needs and expectations, and their complementary self-interest of protecting themselves against the consequences of inadequate or unsatisfactory work; and secondly, to fulfil the need to sustain public confidence by demonstrating a concern for a high standard of professional service and by taking appropriate action to secure it.

As has already been indicated, the regulatory body – whether a professional self-regulatory body or a state regulatory agency – has an interest in this matter. It may be passive, acting against auditors or audit firms only in the event of complaints brought to its notice, and restricting itself to statements of guidance and encouragement to auditors and audit firms to have due regard to the needs of quality control; or it may take an active role, initiating inspection of the work of all auditors and audit firms with a view to providing guidance or imposing penalties for those who are at fault.

There are social and political considerations as well as professional considerations involved in how positive and punitive the external monitoring of the auditing profession should be. The emphasis of the external review system can vary from being largely educational and supportive to assist auditors and audit firms to identify and remedy weaknesses in their own arrangements, to taking a higher profile to create the incentive to improve standards and avoid public reprimand for shortcomings, and to maintain or restore public confidence. A highly active external monitoring system may be necessary in the circumstances of a failure of the profession to maintain standards and a material loss of public confidence; but such a system could be counterproductive by destroying the authority of the profession by the public demonstration of lost confidence in the very essence of professionalism. The system of external review can, however, operate without damage to public confidence, but rather to support public confidence by its reinforcing the measures which the auditors and the audit firms themselves have taken.

Objectives of practice inspection

The external review system may be described as 'practice inspection', 'practice quality review' or 'peer review'.

The objectives of practice inspection or review are to determine whether a reviewed firm's system of quality control is appropriately comprehensive and suitably designed for the firm, whether its quality control policies and procedures are adequately documented and communicated to professional personnel, and whether they are being complied with so as to provide the firm with a reasonable assurance of conforming with professional standards. The principle is that auditing firms obtain a responsible, informed and objective view of whether their auditing practice is being conducted in full accordance with established professional standards. Distinguishing features are that it is the firm that is subject to inspection,[1] the inspection is conducted in the normal course of events, that is, in the absence of any allegation of violation of professional standards, and the inspection is directed principally to the firm's policy and procedures for quality control and their operation rather than to the conduct of particular audit engagements.

Staffing of practice inspection

The inspection/review may be carried out by:

(a) full-time staff of the regulatory or professional body;

(b) full-time staff of the regulatory/professional body supplemented by staff seconded from professional firms for the review;

(c) staff seconded from professional firms on request by the body responsible for the review;

(d) another audit firm ('firm on firm review').

There are advantages and disadvantages to each of these. Full-time staff of the professional or regulatory body may be seen to be more detached, objective and independent, and with no self-interest in a competitor's client files; but they may be thought to be insufficiently familiar with the practice issues with which they are dealing. In a 'firm on firm' review the review staff may be expected to be more familiar with the practice issues but may be thought by outsiders to be too sympathetic to practice problems, and by the reviewed to have an unwelcome access to client files. Where the emphasis of practice inspection is educational and service to members of the profession, full-time staff of a professional body may be thought to be more appropriate and also more cost-effective.

Practice inspection reports

The practice inspection reports will, of course, be sent to the firms inspected and to the body responsible for practice inspection. Since a primary objective is the enhancement of public confidence, the question arises as to whether the reports should be open to public inspection. If practice inspection has been introduced because of a material loss of confidence, there can be little doubt that inspection reports including comments on shortcomings and the report of action taken by the reviewed firms and by the regulatory body should be on file with public access. It is an important contributory factor to public confidence that the monitoring system should be seen to be operating. If practice inspection is a final stage in the system of quality control, where the circumstances are that the regulatory system is seen to be working satisfactorily and there is in general no public complaint with auditing standards, the argument may not be so strong, but the public filing of reports would still seem to be desirable.

Practice inspection, frequency and cost

Practice inspection involves additional audit cost, which requires to be considered in relation to the benefit and value to the public which it produces. Auditors and audit firms have a professional obligation of due care, which requires proper measures to secure the highest standards of professional work. However, cost-benefit considerations apply in auditing. The reduction of risk involves cost, total elimination of risk is impossible, and there is a stage at which the cost of raising the level of confidence is disproportionate to the benefit. It is not possible to lay down specific criteria to cover all sets of circumstances. However, where the auditing profession is of high repute and in good standing in the community, the educational and other admission standards are high, the monitoring and disciplinary procedures are rigorous and effective, and the quality control policies and procedures in auditing firms including final pre-signing review, post-audit review, and inter-office review are well conceived and efficiently applied, then, except in the event of serious complaint, systematic external practice inspection is unlikely to be seen to be required more often than at intervals of a number of years. Any shortcomings on any of these premises would require the extension of the practice inspection programme to be reconsidered.

Responsibility for practice inspection

The impact on public confidence in auditing is a major factor in the consideration of practice inspection. Public perception of its operation and effectiveness is important. A failure to convince the public that practice inspection was ensuring the maintenance of high standards in auditing, improving performance and exposing shortcomings would mean that a principal objective had not been achieved. The firms involved would perhaps derive benefits, and standards would be improved. This would be valuable but of limited value if public confidence was not correspondingly enhanced. It has to be determined, therefore, whether the method of organising practice inspection will have an effect on public perception. If practice inspection is necessary for the maintenance of public confidence in auditing standards, is it essential for the inspection to be conducted and controlled independently of the profession which is being examined? If, for example, there were doubts about public confidence in auditing standards – particularly if there were a crisis of confidence – would that confidence be likely to be restored and sustained by firm on firm review?

As has already been noted, no system of auditing standards, recommendations and guidelines, review or inspection will eliminate the possibility of human failure or guarantee to the public that mistakes will not be made. Public expectations of the reassurance of the audit tend to go beyond what is realistically possible, and in the event of an audit failure there is likely to be criticism not only of the standard of the audit but of the adequacy of the system of quality control. While in the short term the profession is likely to receive credit for its efforts to maintain standards by a system of practice inspection organised by the professional bodies, there is a danger that in the longer term that system could lose credibility and be subject to the criticism – however unjustified – that it was insufficiently rigorous and that the members may be expected to close ranks to protect the profession against public claims of failing to serve the public interest. This potential criticism could be countered, at least partly, by the professional bodies placing the system of practice inspection under the control of a group of non-auditors of public standing and reputation.

As long as there is confidence in the profession there is likely to be confidence in practice inspection organised by the profession, which has safeguards to ensure the independence of the system, and confidence in the capacity of that system to identify weaknesses and improve standards. If, however, there is a real crisis of confidence in auditing standards and audit authority, there must be serious doubts whether confidence can be restored except by a more independent review system. The real public dilemma is that if the profession cannot be relied on to audit others, how can it be relied on to audit itself?

This dilemma serves to underline the critical importance of the profession's retaining public confidence in its professionalism, competence, independence, standards of excellence and a quality control system which is supportive of these ideals.

Postscript

I no longer have a record of the source of the information, but I have among my papers a note that:

Statutes of Westminster in the reign of Edward I refer to auditors as 'officers of importance'.

I believe that the importance of the auditor has never been greater. I hope that this text may contribute to an understanding of the importance of the auditor's role.

Notes

Chapter 1

1. In the United Kingdom, following the adoption by the Council of The European Communities of the EEC Fourth Directive on Company Law in 1978, consideration was given to the question whether 'small' companies which were required by law to have an audit of their accounts should be relieved of that obligation in terms of the discretion granted by that Directive. The proposal was that, instead, the accounts of these companies should be subject to a 'review'. The implication is that 'review' is different from 'audit'. This presupposes that what an audit is is well understood. Some of the problems in the proposal which were highlighted in discussion related to the difficulty of conveying to the user of accounts what a 'review' is and what benefit or reassurance it produces for the user. While the presupposition about the understanding of the meaning of audit may not be well founded and it is unclear what a review is, it appears that it was believed that, at least, review could be distinguished as being different from an audit.

   No action was taken at this time, but consideration was resumed in 1985 following publication by the Department of Trade and Industry of a consultative document on *Accounting and Audit Requirements for Small Firms*. The alternative of 'an independent review' of the accounts which would be less rigorous than an audit was again canvassed. Again, it was decided to make no change.

2. An operational audit is intended to provide a measure of the achievement of an organisation towards its goals and objectives. It is an extension of the internal auditing function into almost all aspects of an organisation's operation and can be viewed as a control technique that provides management with a method for evaluating the effectiveness of operating procedures and internal controls. It is

174

concerned with overall goal achievement, the effectiveness of operating procedures and internal controls, the performance of individual managers, and non-financial as well as financial aspects of the operation of an organisation.
3. A comprehensive examination, analysis and evaluation by an independent external auditor of the performance of management in regard to the objectives, plans, procedures and strategies of the business enterprise or other organisation, and the expression of an opinion on the effectiveness of management in performance of its responsibilities.
4. Acquiring resources in appropriate quality and quantity at the lowest cost.
5. Obtaining maximum useful output from the resources devoted to an activity; utilising minimum resources necessary to achieve a required output or objective; or adopting the policy or course of action to achieve a required objective which requires least input of resources.
6. Success in achieving the objective of the policy or course of action as a consequence of the input of resources.
7. Social audit has to do with social responsibility and monitoring the way in which an organisation conducts itself in its various relationships with society – as employer, manufacturer, supplier, member of the community, etc.

Chapter 2

1. Introducing their proposals for the postulates of auditing, Mautz and Sharaf (1961) quote from Aristotle (*The Thirteen Books of Euclid's Elements*, translated by Sir Thomas L. Heath, vol. 1, second edition, p. 119): 'Every demonstrative science must start from indemonstrable principles, otherwise steps of demonstration would be endless.'
2. For further information and discussion see, for example, Michael G. Sheldon, *Medical Audit in General Practice* (London, The Royal College of General Practitioners, 1982).
3. For further discussion of 'a true and fair view' see David Flint, *A True and Fair View in Company Accounts* (London, Gee, 1982).
4. A research study commissioned by the AICPA Commission on Auditors' Responsibilities resulted in the publication of a report which, the Commission suggested, identified a number of promising approaches for analysing costs and benefits from the point of view of the economy as a whole, of the individual audit client, and of the auditor. See Melvin F. Shakun, *Cost Benefit Analysis of Auditing, Commission on Auditors' Responsibilities Research Study No. 3* (New York: American Institute of Certified Public Accountants, 1978).

Chapter 3

1. The Eighth Directive of the European Commission (84/253/EEC:OJ No. L126, 12.5.1984) deals with the qualifications of persons responsible for auditing the annual accounts of companies and firms, and recognises 'the high level of theoretical knowledge required for the statutory auditing of accounting documents'. It prescribes a common standard of education and training for persons who may be approved as auditors. They must attain university entrance level, complete a course of theoretical instruction, undergo practical training for a minimum of three years, and pass an examination of professional competence at final university level recognised by the state. The subjects of theoretical study and of practical training are prescribed and certain conditions of practical training are also stipulated.

Chapter 4

1. Effect on the financial position of a person with whom the auditor has a personal relationship must also be considered. For example, investments held by a spouse, child, parent, or partner, borrowing or lending by any of these, or interest in a trust by any of these, are potentially objectionable. Where the auditor has knowledge of such involvement of an employee, close friend or co-director this position may also need to be considered.
2. It is not intended to suggest that an auditor can act without impartiality and objectivity; what is being discussed is the extent of his or her exposure to influence or pressure.

Chapter 6

1. For further discussion of this matter see David J. Hatherly, *The Audit Evidence Process* (London: Anderson Keenan, 1980).

Chapter 7

1. See *London* v. *General Bank (No. 2)* (1895) 2 Ch. 673.
2. See Department of Trade Inspectors, *Report of Investigation under Section 165(b) of the Companies Act 1948 into the affairs of Peachey Property Corporation Ltd* (London: HMSO, 1979), p. 156.

3. For a discussion of the dilemma see Lee J. Seidler, 'Symbolism and Communication in the Auditor's Report', in Howard Stettler (ed.) *Auditing Symposium III; Proceedings of the 1976 Touche Ross/University of Kansas Symposium on Auditing Problems* (Lawrence, Kansas: School of Business, University of Kansas, 1976), pp. 32–44.

Chapter 8

1. For further discussion of materiality, see T. Lee, *Materiality, An Audit Brief* (London: Auditing Practices Committee of the Consultative Committee of Accountancy Bodies, 1984), and Donald A. Leslie, *Materiality: The Concept and its Application to Auditing, a Research Study* (Toronto, Canada: The Canadian Institute of Chartered Accountants, 1985).

Chapter 10

1. The Union Européenne des Experts Comptables Economiques et Financiers ceased to exist and was replaced by the Fédération des Experts Comptables Européens (FEE) with effect from 1 January 1987.
2. The Local Government Finance Act 1982 which established the Audit Commission for Local Authorities in England and Wales provided (Section 14) that 'The Commission shall prepare, and keep under review a code of audit practice, prescribing the way in which auditors are to carry out their functions' under the Act; that 'The code shall embody what appears to the Commission to be the best professional practice with respect to the standards, procedures and techniques to be adopted by auditors'; and that 'The code shall not come into force until approved by a resolution of each House of Parliament'. It is under this authority that the Commission has prepared a Code of Local Government Audit Practice for England and Wales.
3. The Institute of Chartered Accountants in England and Wales; The Institute of Chartered Accountants of Scotland; The Institute of Chartered Accountants in Ireland; The Chartered Association of Certified Accountants; The Chartered Institute of Public Finance and Accountancy.

Chapter 11

1. For a report on experience in Canada, where individual members are inspected, see David A. Wilson, *Practice Inspection: Weaving a Strong New Thread into the Professional Fabric*, Arthur Young Lecture No. 8 (Glasgow: Department of Accountancy, School of Financial Studies, University of Glasgow, 1986).

References

AAA, *Studies in Accounting Research No. 6: A Statement of Basic Auditing Concepts* (Sarasota: American Accounting Association, 1973) p. 2.

AICPA, *Statement on Auditing Standards No. 1* (New York: American Institute of Certified Public Accountants, 1973) p. 1.

AICPA, *Report, Conclusions and Recommendations of The Commission on Auditors' Responsibilities* (The Cohen Commission) (New York: American Institute of Certified Public Accountants, 1978) p. xii.

AICPA, 'Restructuring Professional Standards to Achieve Professional Excellence in a Changing Environment', *Report of the Special Committee on Standards of Professional Conduct for Certified Public Accountants* (New York: American Institute of Certified Public Accountants, 1986) p. 15.

Barradell, M., *Ethics and the Accountant* (London: Gee, 1969).

Burton, J. C., 'Symposium on Ethics in Corporate Financial Reporting', *Journal of Accountancy*, January 1972.

CICA, *Report of the Special Committee to Examine the Role of the Auditor* (Toronto: Canadian Institute of Chartered Accountants, 1978) para. B3.

Department of Trade Inspectors, *Report of Investigation under Section 165(b) of the Companies Act 1948 into the Affairs of Peachey Property Corporation Ltd* (London: HMSO, 1979) p. 24.

Dickerson, R. W. V., *Accountants and the Law of Negligence* (Canada: Canadian Institute of Chartered Accountants, 1966).

Gilling, D. M., 'Auditors and their Role in Society – the Legal Concept of Status', *Australian Business Law Review*, June 1976.

HM Government, *The Role of the Comptroller and Auditor General*, Green Paper presented to Parliament by the Chancellor of the Exchequer, Cmnd 7845 (London: HMSO, 1980) p. 8.

ICAEW, ICAS, ICAI, CACA and CIPFA, *Auditing Standards and Guidelines, Explanatory Foreword* (London and Edinburgh: The

Institute of Chartered Accountants in England and Wales, The Institute of Chartered Accountants of Scotland, The Institute of Chartered Accountants in Ireland, The Chartered Association of Certified Accountants, The Chartered Institute of Public Finance and Accountancy, 1980) para. 2.

IFAC *International Auditing Guidelines: No. 1, Objective and Scope of the Audit of Financial Statements* (New York: International Federation of Accountants, 1980) p. 9.

Limperg, T., *The Social Responsibility of the Auditor* (Amsterdam: Limperg Instituut, 1985).

Mautz, R. K., *The Role of the Independent Auditor in a Market Economy*, unpublished background paper for the AICPA Commission on Auditors' Responsibilities, 1975a.

Mautz, R. K., *The Role of Auditing in Our Society*, unpublished background paper for the AICPA Commission on Auditors' Responsibilities, 1975b.

Mautz, R. K. and Sharaf, H. A., *The Philosophy of Auditing* (Sarasota: American Accounting Association, 1961) pp. 6 and 10.

Metcalf Committee, *Report of the Sub-committee on Reports, Accounting and Management of the Committee on Governmental Affairs United States Senate* (*Journal of Accountancy*, January 1978) p. 90.

Normanton, E. L., *The Accountability and Audit of Governments* (Manchester: Manchester University Press, 1966).

Tricker, R. I., 'Corporate Accountability and the Role of the Audit Function', in A. G. Hopwood, M. Bromwich and J. Shaw (eds) *Auditing Research: Issues and Opportunities* (London: Pitman, 1982).

Index

181